Rapid Assessment Program

8

RAP
Working
Papers

A Rapid Assessment of the Humid Forests of South Central Chuquisaca, Bolivia

CONSERVATION INTERNATIONAL

RAP Working Papers are published by:
Conservation International
Department of Conservation Biology
2501 M Street, NW, Suite 200
Washington, DC 20037
USA
202-429-5660
202-887-0193 fax
www.conservation.org

Editors:
Thomas S. Schulenberg
Kim Awbrey
Assistant Editor: Glenda Fabregas
Design: KINETIK Communication Graphics, Inc.
Maps: Carmen Reed
Cover photograph: Louise H. Emmons
Translations: Enrique Ortiz

ISBN 1-881173-19-4

**Schulenberg, T. S., and K. Awbrey (Eds.).
1997. A rapid assessment of the humid forests of South Central Chuquisaca, Bolivia. RAP Working Papers 8, Conservation International.**

✪ Printed on recycled paper

This publication has been funded in part by CI-USAID Cooperative Agreement #PCE-5554-A-00-4020-00.

TABLE OF CONTENTS

PARTICIPANTS

SURVEY STAFF

Bruce K. Holst
Marie Selby Botanical Gardens

Luzmilla Arroyo Padilla
Museo de Historia Natural
"Noel Kempff Mercado"

Martha Serrano
Plan Agroforestal de Chuquisaca, Sucre

Michael B. Harvey
University of Texas at Arlington

Fernando Guerra
Colección Boliviana de Fauna

Thomas S. Schulenberg
Conservation International

Carmen Quirroga O.
Colección Boliviana de Fauna

Louise H. Emmons
U.S. National Museum of Natural History

COORDINATORS

Lois Jammes
Armonía

Alan Hesse
Armonía

Kim Awbrey
Conservation International

EDITORS

Thomas S. Schulenberg
Kim Awbrey
Conservation International

ACKNOWLEDGEMENTS

We thank Los Palmereños, the people of El Palmar, for their interest in and support of our field studies. The expedition would not have been possible without the expertise and logistical wizardry of Lois Jammes and his staff, particularly Alan Hesse and Mincho, at Fundación Armonía of Santa Cruz. We are indebted to the Dirección Nacional de la Conservación de la Biodiversidad, especially Alexandra Sanchez de Lozada and Eliana Flores, for their collaboration and for their support of our work in Chuquisaca.

We also would like to thank our partners in the Global Bureau for the Environment at USAID, particularly Cynthia Gill and Jerry Bisson, as well as Mike Yates at the USAID mission in La Paz. The expedition to El Palmar, and the publication of this report, were funded by USAID through a cooperative agreement with CI. We also would like to thank the W. Alton Jones Foundation for their support, especially for sponsoring the series of overflights that preceded the expedition, and for their ongoing dedication to further understanding and conservation of the tropical Andes.

Jon Fjeldså and Sjoerd Mayer provided maps and unpublished manuscripts describing their own field surveys in Chuquisaca. This material was useful to our expedition, and we are grateful for their courtesy.

The North Face, Inc. generously donated field equipment for the RAP expedition; we are very grateful for this assistance.

We thank the following specialists for their assistance in identifying botanical specimens: Bruce Allen (Bryophytes), Paul Berry (Onagraceae), Germán Carnival (Orchidaceae), Thomas Croat (Araceae), William D'Arcy (Solanaceae), Gerrit Davidse (Cyperaceae, Poaceae), Roy Gereau (Rosaceae), Ronald Liesner (miscellaneous), Harry Luther (Bromeliaceae), Peter Jorgenson (Passifloraceae), James Miller (Boraginaceae), G. Navarro (Meliaceae), Harold Robinison (Asteraceae), Alan R. Smith (Pteridophytes), James Solomon (Cactaceae, Vitaceae), Charlotte Taylor (Rubiaceae), Roberto Vasquez (Orchidaceae), Bruno Wallnöfer (Dioscoreaceae), Henk van der Werff (Lauraceae), and John Wurdack (Melastomataceae). Thanks also to James Solomon for providing a copy of his unpublished notes on Tarija forests. For help and suggestions on the identification of mammal specimens, we thank M. Carleton, A. L. Gardner, P. Myers, and M. de Vivo.

And special thanks to our partners in the Rapid Assessment Program in the office of Environmental and Conservation Programs, under the direction of Dr. Debra Moskovits at the Field Museum of Natural History, for their dedication to this project. Our work also would not have been possible without the support of the staff at CI-Bolivia, especially Ana Maria Martinet de Molinedo and Guillermo Rioja.

OVERVIEW

VISIÓN GENERAL

INTRODUCTION
(Thomas S. Schulenberg, Bruce K. Holst, Robin B. Foster and Louise H. Emmons)

Wet forests, in Bolivia usually termed "Yungas" forests, cover the eastern slopes of the Andes from Venezuela to northern Argentina. South of where the Andes make their dramatic bend in the Department of Santa Cruz, Bolivia, within the Bolivian departments of Chuquisaca and Tarija, is probably the most dramatic shift in flora and vegetation anywhere along the entire eastern slope of the Andes. But biological information for this region, especially in Chuquisaca, has remained very sketchy.

The southern extreme of the Yungas forests, from south-central Bolivia south to northwestern Argentina, contains a distinctive assemblage of plant species. These forests, a subset of the Yungas, often are designated as Bosque Tucumano-Boliviano or Tucuman-Bolivian forest. Bosques Tucumano-Boliviano are less diverse than are more northern Yungas, but still contain a number of endemic plant species and represent 1 of the 14 major vegetation types recognized in Bolivia (Beck et al. 1993). This region also includes recognizable areas of endemism for small mammals (this report) and of birds (Cracraft 1985, Stotz et al. 1996).

The current condition of Bosques Tucumano-Boliviano, and of other biological communities in southern Bolivia, are important immediate ques-

INTRODUCCIÓN
(Thomas S. Schulenberg, Bruce K. Holst, Robin B. Foster y Louise H. Emmons)

Los bosques húmedos, frecuentemente llamados bosques "Yungas" en Bolivia, cubren las vertientes orientales de los Andes desde Venezuela hasta el norte de Argentina. Al sur de donde los Andes hacen una curva dramática en el Departamento de Santa Cruz, Bolivia, dentro de los Departamentos Bolivianos de Chuquisaca y Tarija, está probablemente el cambio más dramático en la flora y la vegetación que en cualquier otra parte de la vertiente oriental de los Andes. Pero la información biológica para esta región, especialmente en Chuquisaca, ha permanecido muy escasa.

El extremo sur de los bosques Yungas, desde el sur central de Bolivia, y al sur hasta el noroeste de Argentina, contiene una composición de especies de plantas distintiva. Estos bosques, una sub-categoría de los Yungas, son a menudo designados como Bosque Tucumano-Boliviano. Los Bosques Tucumano-Bolivianos son menos diversos en comparación con los bosques Yungas más al norte, pero aun así contienen una cantidad considerable de especies de plantas endémicas y representan uno de los catorce principales tipos de vegetación reconocidos en Bolivia (Beck et al. 1993). Esta región también incluye áreas reconocidas por su endemismo de especies de mamíferos pequeños (este reporte) y de aves (Cracraft 1985, Stotz et al. 1996).

tions for conservation. During a series of over-flights over the southern Andes of Bolivia, from 1 to 3 November 1994, members of the RAP team (R. Foster, T. Schulenberg, L. H. Emmons, L. Jammes, D. Moskovits, and I. Vargas) were able to survey from the air most of the easternmost slopes of the Andes from the southern end of Parque Nacional Amboró south to southern Tarija. We located the southernmost extensions of the Andean tropical-wet forest in Bolivia and identified the topographic-climatic conditions that maintain them.

The topography of most of the Department of Chuquisaca is characterized by a series of steep parallel ridges that run north/south. These ridges are separated by flat-bottomed valleys. Most of these ridges are less than 1500 m and contain dry, Serrano Chaqueño vegetation on their slopes. The bottoms of these valleys largely have been converted to pasture. To the east, beyond the last ridge, lies the vast, flat Chaco thorn-forest. To the west, the straight ridges end at a higher "wall" that extends up to 3000 m and marks the edge of the main Andean massif. On the top of this massif is the broad Bolivian altiplano and the capital city, Sucre. At intervals this wall is penetrated by the major river valleys, with their much more convoluted topography, that drain the core Andes. This is the area where the best stands remaining in Bolivia of Bosque Tucumano-Boliviano exist. This also is the "subcontinental divide," with some of these rivers veering north to the Amazon drainage and others south to the Río Paraná.

The broad band of wet Yungas forest, which is fairly continuous on the Andean slopes to the north, becomes fragmented after the Santa Cruz bend, just south of the Parque Nacional Amboró. The original pattern of vegetation here is obscured by the alteration associated with the major highway that connects the city of Santa Cruz to Cochabamba and Sucre, and by the extensive colonization around the town of Valle Grande. However, the general pattern is clear even here, and throughout Chuquisaca to the south: the wet forest continues only on the ridges that are high enough for clouds to form or to hit consistently during much of the year. These areas may not receive much rainfall in the dry season,

La condición actual de los Bosques Tucumano-Boliviano, y de otras comunidades biológicas en el sur de Bolivia, constituyen interrogantes importantes y urgentes para la conservación. Durante una serie de sobrevuelos sobre el sur de los Andes Bolivianos, desde el 1 hasta el 3 de noviembre de 1994, los miembros del equipo RAP (R. Foster, T. Schulenberg, L. H. Emmons, L. Jammes, D. Moskovits, y I. Vargas) pudieron muestrear desde el aire la mayoría de vertientes más orientales de los Andes desde el extremo sur del Parque Nacional Amboró al sur, hasta el sur de Tarija. Hemos localizado las extensiones más sureñas de los bosques tropical-húmedo Andinos en Bolivia y hemos identificado las condiciones climático-topográficas que los mantienen.

La topografía de la mayor parte del departamento de Chuquisaca está caracterizada por una serie de crestas empinadas paralelas que van de norte a sur. Estas crestas están separadas por valles de fondo plano. La mayoría de estas crestas son menores de 1500 m y contienen una vegetación seca, Serrana Chaqueña en sus laderas. Los fondos de estos valles han sido convertido a pastizales en su mayor parte. Hacia el este, más allá de la última cresta, está el extenso y plano Bosque Espinoso Chaqueño. Hacia el oeste, las crestas rectas terminan en una "pared" más alta que se extiende hasta los 3000 m y que marca el borde del macizo Andino principal. En la cima de este macizo está el extenso altiplano Boliviano y la ciudad capital, Sucre. A intervalos, esta "pared" está penetrada por los valles de los ríos principales, con su topografía mucho más complicada, que desaguan los Andes centrales. Esta es el área en Bolivia donde existen las mejores áreas que quedan de los bosques Tucumano-Bolivianos. Esta es también la "divisoria subcontinental", con algunos de los ríos dirigiéndose hacia el norte a la cuenca Amazónica y con otros hacia el sur al río Paraná.

La ancha banda de bosques Yungas húmedos, la cual es regularmente contínua en las laderas Andinas hacia el norte, se fragmenta después de la curva de Santa Cruz, inmediatamente al sur del Parque Nacional Amboró. El patrón original de la vegetación está aquí confundido por la alteración asociada con la carretera principal que conecta la ciudad de Santa Cruz con Cochabamba y Sucre, y

This is the area where the best stands remaining in Bolivia of Bosque Tucumano-Boliviano exist.

but they can extract considerable moisture from the clouds through condensation on the vegetation. This is analogous to the fog-forests of central California that permit the survival of Sequoias even with long summers without rain.

The most extensive ridges supporting clouds are the "wall" escarpment referred to above and the ridges, usually high, that are adjacent to it. Any ridge over 1500 m seems to have at least some variant of wet forest, although the elevation at which it occurs may vary up to a couple hundred meters. The Yungas forest only occurs up to about 2500 m because of the increasingly drier conditions above that elevation, and because fires, set by the human population of the highlands, continue to burn lower and lower. Consequently, there is only a very narrow band, of about 1000 m, of Yungas vegetation in Chuquisaca.

The southernmost block of what was once apparently a near-continuous band of Andean wet forest lies against the Andean escarpment between the ríos Pilcomayo and Pilaya. There may be some similar vegetation further south and west in the Department of Tarija, but this is well separated from the rest of the Yungas.

Since the strips of wet Yungas vegetation of the outlier ridges to the east are much smaller in area and more isolated, they are expected to have a much more reduced subset of the wet-forest species than the areas on or adjacent to the slopes of the wall. These outliers may also be more subject to extreme years of unusual drought. However, one cannot discard the idea that they may sometimes be refuges for otherwise rare or unusual species.

The lower slopes of most of the ridges and most of the floodplains are covered with deciduous dry forest, which thus is the dominant vegetation of eastern Chuquisaca. This forest or some variant of it extends into the core Andes on the slopes of the river valleys that penetrate the wall. It is these valleys that more accurately fit the concept of "inter-Andean dry valleys," rather than the rows of shallow valleys characteristic of eastern Chuquisaca. The dry forest appeared to be most heterogeneous near the wall where the underlying geological diversity and greater availability of

por la colonización extensiva alrededor de la ciudad de Valle Grande. Sin embargo, el patrón general está claro inclusive aquí y a lo largo de Chuquisaca hacia el sur: el bosque húmedo continua solo sobre las crestas que son lo suficientemente altas para que se formen nubes o que estas choquen consistentemente durante la mayor parte del año. Estas áreas pueden no recibir mucha lluvia en la estación seca, pero pueden extraer humedad considerable de las nubes a través de la condensación sobre la vegetación. Esto es análogo con los bosques de neblina de California central que permiten la sobrevivencia de los Sequoias aún con largos veranos sin lluvia.

La crestas más extensas que mantienen a las nubes son la "pared" escarpada mencionada anteriormente, y las crestas, frecuentemente altas, que están adyacentes a ella. Cada cresta encima de los 1500 m parece albergar por lo menos alguna variante de bosque húmedo, aunque la elevación en los cuales estos aparecen puede variar hasta por un par de cientos de metros. El bosque de Yungas se encuentra solamente hasta los 2500 m, a causa de una creciente disminución de la humedad sobre esa altitud y también por los incendios producidos por los pobladores del altiplano, que continúan incendiando áreas más y más bajas. En consecuencia, queda solamente una franja muy angosta, de cerca de 1000 m, de vegetación Yunga en Chuquisaca.

El bloque más sureño de lo que aparentemente fuera alguna vez una franja casi continua de bosque Andino húmedo queda al frente del escarpado Andino entre los ríos Pilcomayo y Pilaya. Es probable que exista alguna vegetación similar más al sur y oeste en el Departamento de Tarija, pero esto está bien separado del resto de las Yungas.

Dado que las franjas de la vegetación Yunga húmeda de las crestas adyacentes hacia el este son mucho más pequeñas en área y también más aisladas, es de esperar que ellas tengan una submuestra mucho lá reducida de las especies de bosque húmedo que otras áreas encima de, o contiguas a las laderas de la "pared." Esos relictos pueden estar también más afectados por los años con sequías excepcionales. Sin embargo, uno no puede descartar la idea que ellos puedan servir de refugio para otras especies raras o inusuales.

Los laderas bajas de la mayoría de las crestas y

The forests of Chuquisaca are being destroyed both from above and below.

1

2

3

4

5

6

1. Northeast corner of Bufete escarpment

2. Humid forest understory, on ridge above Limón

3. Forested ridge north of Cerro Bufete

4. Humid forest, base of Cerro Bufete escarpment

5. Dwarf forest, Cerro Tigrecillos summit

6. Gallery forests on summit of Cerro Bufete

7. Forest camp at Limón, Río Santa Martha

8. *Lutreolina*, an aquatic opossum captured at Bufete

9. Headwaters of Río Limonal, below Cerro Bufete

10. Río Santa Marta

11. Río Pilcomayo near El Palmar

12. Wall of Bufete escarpment

13. Canyon wall of upper Río Limonal

14. Grazed pastures on summit of Cerro Bufete

15. Río Limonal cascading off Cerro Bufete

16. Northeast corner of Cerro Bufete

17. Bufete escarpment, looking north

18. Dome on summit of Cerro Bufete

19. Pastures at El Palmar

20. El Palmar, from the air

21. Protective wall of *Yucca* around garden, El Palmar

22. El Palmar, viewed from slopes of Bufete

7

8

9

10

11

12

13

14

15

16

17

18

19

20

21

22

CONSERVATION INTERNATIONAL

Rapid Assessment Program

underground water may be having an effect.

The other distinct vegetation observed was in the broadest, flattest valley bottoms in the south. Here there appear to be extensive stands of chaco-like thorn-forest. If that is what they are, these islands of chaco vegetation might be very useful in teaching us the ecological basis for what makes the chaco such a distinctive habitat.

The view from the overflights dramatically highlighted the long-term conditions of the forests visible below us: the forests of Chuquisaca are being destroyed both from above and below. The highest elevation band of these forests is burned by the residents of the altiplano as they move down the escarpment. The tops of the outlier ridges to the east also are being burned by residents of the lowland, to create dry-season pasture. The colonization in the valleys follows the rivers and roads and then moves up slope.

This colonization pressure, both from above and from below, has left few large areas of forest areas remaining. Virtually all the valleys in this region already have some colonization. The largest blocks of dry forest, with the least amount of human intervention, are in the southeast, for example, in the area west of Villamontes where the Río Pilcomayo emerges onto the Chaco. For wet Yungas vegetation and a variety of other habitats, we found only two large blocks of forest that remain. Both of these are adjacent to the escarpment, and even these are something less than pristine. One is east of Padilla along a section of the Río Grande. The other forest is further south, between the ríos Pilcomayo and the Pilaya, west of El Palmar (20°51'S, 64°19'W). The larger, and more remote of these areas, by El Palmar, was chosen as the site for a RAP survey.

SUMMARY OF RESULTS
(Louise H. Emmons, Michael B. Harvey, Bruce K. Holst and Thomas S. Schulenberg)

During May 1995, an interdisciplinary team of nine biologists surveyed semi-humid forests to the west of El Palmar, in south-central Chuquisaca, Bolivia. The survey area contains

también la mayoría de las áreas inundables están cubiertas por bosque caducifolio seco, el cual es en consecuencia la vegetación dominante de Chuquisaca oriental. Este bosque o alguna variante del mismo, se extiende hacia los Andes centrales sobre las laderas de los valles de los ríos que penetran la "pared." Estos son los valles que más o menos encajan en el concepto de "valles secos inter-Andinos", más que las franjas de valles poco profundos característicos de Chuquisaca oriental. El bosque seco pareció ser más heterogéneo cerca de la "pared" donde la diversidad geológica subyacente y la mayor disponibilidad del agua subterránea pueden tener algún efecto.

La otra vegetación más distinta observada estuvo en los valles de fondos más anchos y planos en el sur. Allí parecen haber unos extensos bosques espinosos parecidos al bosque Chaqueño. Si esto es lo que son, estas islas de vegetación de chaco pueden ser muy útil para enseñarnos la base ecológica de lo que hace al chaco un hábitat tan especial.

La vista desde los sobrevuelos resaltó dramáticamente las condiciones a largo plazo del bosque visible debajo de nosotros: los bosques de Chuquisaca continúan siendo destruidos tanto por arriba como por abajo. La franja de altitud más alta de estos bosques continua siendo quemada por los residentes del altiplano mientras van bajando del macizo. Las cumbres de las crestas adyacentes hacia el este están también siendo quemadas por los residentes de las zonas bajas para crear pastizales para la estación seca. La colonización en las valles sigue los ríos y carreteras y después continua hacia arriba por las laderas.

Esta presión de colonización, tanto de arriba como de abajo, ha dejado pocas áreas grandes del bosque. Casi todos las valles en este región ya tienen algún nivel de colonización. Los bloques más grandes de bosque seco, con el grado más pequeño de intervención humana, están en el sureste, por ejemplo, en el área al oeste de Villamontes donde el Río Pilcomayo emerge sobre el Chaco. De el tipo de vegetación Yunga húmeda y otras variedades de hábitats, hemos encontrado que solamente quedan dos bloques grandes de bosque. Ambos están adyacentes al escarpado, y aún estos están algo menos que prístinos. Uno está al este de Padilla a lo largo de una sección del Río

Los bosques de Chuquisaca continúan siendo destruidos tanto por arriba como por abajo.

one of the largest remaining tracts of Bosque Tucumano-Boliviano. Three sites were explored by the team (see gazetteer and itinerary): the slopes and summit (2580 m) of Cerro Bufete, to the west of El Palmar; the middle Río Santa Martha valley, to the north of El Palmar; and slopes and summit (2150 m) of Cerro Tigrecillos, along the upper Río Santa Martha. The highest altitudes were reached on Cerro Bufete and Cerro Tigrecillos.

Biological diversity in the area was somewhat higher than we had expected. We were surprised to find that most of the forests were severely disturbed, however, in ways that were not visible from our overflights, and would not register on satellite images. Regular human disturbance including grazing of cattle, an invasion by feral *Citrus* trees, and, to a lesser extent, logging. If present trends continue, these forests will suffer a slow, continuous decline. Probably it is too late to control the spread of *Citrus*, but it may be possible to develop management plans that would reduce the potential for damage from fire, grazing and logging.

The slopes and valley bottoms from about 1300 to 1900 m were covered in a fairly tall (15-25 m) forest that was dominated in most areas by either *Siphoneugena* or *Myrcianthes* (both Myrtaceae). Other elements in these forests were species of Lauraceae, *Blepharocalyx* (Myrtaceae), *Parapiptadenia* (Mimosaceae), *Tabebuia* (Bignoniaceae), *Crinodendron* (Elaeocarpaceae), *Cedrela* (Meliaceae), *Juglans* (Juglandaceae) and *Trichilia* (Meliaceae). These forests commonly contained pockets of 3-7 m tall tree ferns and had a high abundance of epiphytes (mostly pteridophytes and bryophytes). Ridge tops and plateaus between 1800 and 2200 m that we visited had low (5-15 m tall) forests composed mostly of *Ilex* (Aquifoliaceae), *Viburnum* (Caprifoliaceae), *Prunus* (Rosaceae), *Clethra* (Clethraceae), *Myrsine* (Myrsinaceae), *Roupala* (Proteaceae) and *Symplocos* (Symplocaceae). Higher altitude, dwarf forests (2000-2500 m) contained some *Podocarpus* (Podocarpaceae), *Alnus* (Betulaceae), *Polylepis* (Rosaceae) and *Berberis* (Berberidaceae).

Signs of human disturbance were evident in most areas that we visited. The two most signifi-

Grande. El otro queda más al sur, entre los ríos Pilcomayo y Pilaya, al oeste de El Palmar (20°51'S, 64°19'W). De estas dos áreas, la más grande y aislada, El Palmar, fue escogida como el sitio para la evaluación del RAP.

RESUMEN DE LOS RESULTADOS
(Louise H. Emmons, Michael B. Harvey, Bruce K. Holst y Thomas S. Schulenberg)

En mayo de 1995, un equipo interdisciplinario de nueve biólogos hicieron un reconocimiento de un bosque semi-húmedo hacia el oeste de El Palmar, en el sur-central de Chuquisaca, Bolivia. El área del reconocimiento contiene una de los trechos más grandes de Bosque Tucumano-Boliviano que quedan. Tres localidades fueron exploradas por el equipo (ver el gazetteer y el itinerario): las laderas y las cumbres (2580 m) del Cerro Bufete, hasta el oeste de El Palmar; la parte media del valle del Río Santa Martha, hacia el norte de El Palmar; y las laderas y cumbres (2150 m) del Cerro Tigrecillos, a lo largo del alto Río Santa Martha. Se llego a las altitudes más elevadas en el Cerro Bufete y el Cerro Tigrecillos.

La diversidad biológica en el área era un poco más alta de lo que habíamos esperado. Estuvimos sorprendidos de encontrar que la mayor parte de los bosques estaban severamente perturbados, sin embargo, de una manera que no era detectable durante los sobrevuelos, y que no sería registrada en los imágenes de satélite. Estas perturbaciones humanas regulares incluyeron pastoreo de ganado, una invasión de árboles silvestres *Citrus*, y a menor escala, extracción de madera. Si es que estas tendencias actuales se mantienen, estos bosques van a sufrir una lenta y continua degradación. Probablemente ya es muy tarde para poder controlar la dispersion de *Citrus*, pero podría ser posible desarrollar planes de manejo que reducirían el potencial de daños por el fuego, el pastoreo de ganado, y la extracción de madera.

Los laderas y fondos de valles desde alrededor de 1300 hasta 1900 m estuvieron cubiertos por un bosque regularmente alto (15-25 m) que estaba dominado en la mayoría de áreas por

Biological diversity in the area was somewhat higher than we had expected.

cant forms of disturbance were grazing by cattle, and an invasion of feral *Citrus* trees. A third type of disturbance, logging, also was observed on a small scale. A few areas, such as around the village of El Palmar, on the summit of Cerro Bufete, and the ridges running W and N from Bufete, routinely (at least annually) are burned to stimulate new growth of pasture for cattle. Cattle also forage throughout the forests, limited only by areas with very steep slopes or broken terrain with numerous boulders. This activity affects almost all of the forest along the trail between El Palmar and Cerro Bufete, and up to at least 1600 m on Cerro Tigrecillos. We noted much evidence of grazing in the forest understory, but it is not clear how long cattle have been present in the high numbers that currently are typical, nor is it clear what will be the long-term damage to forest species composition that cattle may make. The grazing area on Cerro Bufete is managed by the community of El Palmar, but the Palmareños also have agreements that allow people from other communities from the highlands (Culpina) to use the area for grazing. Several men from the El Palmar area noted a degradation, which they attributed to overgrazing, over recent years in the quality of the pasture on the summit of Cerro Bufete. It should be noted that this region was classified as unsuitable for cattle by the Corporación Regional de Desarrollo de Chuquisaca (Agreda et al. 1994).

The invasion of the forest by *Citrus* is unusual in that *Citrus* normally do not self-seed or spread in areas in which they have been introduced. The original seeds probably were carried into the area by people tending cattle or by subsistence farmers. Fruits are fed upon by animals, such as agoutis, monkeys, and parrots, and possibly also by cattle and tapirs. Dispersal by gravity probably also plays a role. The areas with the highest degrees of *Citrus* infestation were ridge-tops and moist valley floors, areas most often grazed by cattle. In such areas, *Citrus* accounted for up to 45% of all individual trees greater than 10 cm in diameter. Elevation seems to be a limiting factor, as *Citrus* is not found in areas higher than about 1900-2000 m. Apparently Bosques Tucumano-Boliviano in Bolivia are not the only such forests

Siphoneugena o *Myrcianthes* (ambos Myrtaceae). Otros elementos en estos bosques eran las especies de Lauraceae, *Blepharocalyx* (Myrtaceae), *Parapiptadenia* (Mimosaceae), *Tabebuia* (Bignoniaceae), *Crinodendron* (Elaeocarpaceae), *Cedrela* (Meliaceae), *Juglans* (Juglandaceae) y *Trichilia* (Meliaceae). Estos bosques normalmente contenían porciones con helechos arbóreos de 3-7 m de altura, y tenían una alta abundancia de epífitas (principalmente pteridofitas y briofitas). Las cimas de las crestas y las mesetas que visitamos, entre 1800 y 2200 m, tenían bosques de baja estatura (5-15 m de alto) compuestos mayormente de *Ilex* (Aquifoliaceae), *Viburnum* (Caprifoliaceae), *Prunus* (Rosaceae), *Clethra* (Clethraceae), *Myrsine* (Myrsinaceae), *Roupala* (Proteaceae) y *Symplocos* (Symplocaceae). A altitudes mayores (2000-2500 m), los bosques enanos contenían algunos *Podocarpus* (Podocarpaceae), *Alnus* (Betulaceae), *Polylepis* (Rosaceae) y *Berberis* (Berberidaceae).

En la mayoría de áreas que hemos visitado las muestras de perturbaciones humanas fueron evidentes. Las dos formas más significativas de perturbaciones fueron pastoreo de ganado, y la invasión de árboles exóticos asilvestrados de *Citrus*. Un tercer tipo de perturbación, la extracción de madera, también fue observada pero a menor escala. Algunas otras áreas, tales como los alrededores del pueblo de El Palmar, en la cumbre del Cerro Bufete, y las crestas hacia el norte y oeste de Bufete, son rutinariamente quemadas (por lo menos una vez al año) para estimular el rebrotamiento de pastos para el ganado. El ganado también forrajea a lo largo de todos los bosques, limitado solamente en áreas con laderas muy empinadas o terrenos quebrados con numerosos peñascos. Esta actividad afecta casi todos los bosques a lo largo del camino entre El Palmar y el Cerro Bufete, y hacia arriba por lo menos hasta los 1600 m en el Cerro Tigrecillos. Hemos notado mucha evidencia de pastoreo en el sotobosque, pero no es claro desde cuando ha estado el ganado presente en la gran abundancia que ahora es característica, ni tampoco es claro cual será el daño que el ganado pueda ocasionar a largo plazo para la composición de especies del bosque. El área de pastoreo en el Cerro Bufete está manejado por la comunidad de El Palmar, pero los Palmareños también tienen

La diversidad biológica en el área era un poco más alta de lo que habíamos esperado.

with a problematic *Citrus* invasion. One of the most aggressive exotics in the Bosque Tucumano-Boliviano of Parque Nacional El Rey in Salta, Argentina also is *Citrus* (Chalukian 1991).

Logging seems to be conducted only on a small scale with the wood being carried out by mules. Valuable timber trees are *Juglans* and *Cedrela*. Areas farther to the south, which are more accessible by road, are being leased to private companies by the government for future logging. This has caused some fear in El Palmar that the forests close to this village, and which are used by the local community, also will be leased to outside companies.

On two separate overflights (22 May 1995) we surveyed the landscape in an area from just south of Cerro Bufete north to Cerro Tigrecillos. Clearings could be seen near the lower portions of all river valleys, and in the Limonal and Cochayo basins a few clearings were seen higher up the valley. The Río Santa Martha valley, above the area in which we camped at El Limón, was not visibly disturbed. There probably are some cattle wandering into the more accessible areas, however, especially on the south side of the river. We saw numerous landslides on the steep slopes in this basin.

Over a quarter of the bird species recorded at El Palmar and at the two field sites previously were unknown, or only recently were recorded, for the department. Many of these new records fill in "holes" in the distribution of species previously known from localities both to the north (Santa Cruz) and to the south (Tarija or Argentina). Several species, such as *Scytalopus bolivianus* (Southern White-crowned Tapaculo), *Mionectes striaticollis* (Streak-necked Flycatcher), *Chlorophonia cyanea* (Blue-naped Chlorophonia), *Anisognathus flavinucha* (Blue-winged Mountain-Tanager), and *Piranga leucoptera* (White-winged Tanager) that were encountered during the survey represent new southern records. These species all are typical of humid montane forest, and suggest that the forests near El Palmar are more humid and more diverse than the better-known forests in Tarija.

The most important ornithological discovery was of a population of *Cinclus schulzi* (Rufous-

acuerdos para permitir el uso para pastoreo por personas de otras comunidades de zonas más altas (Culpina). Varios hombres de El Palmar notaron la degradación en la calidad de los pastos de las cumbres del Cerro Bufete en los últimos años, la cual atribuyeron al sobrepastoreo. Debe recolcarse que esta región fue clasificada como inapropiada para el pastoreo por la Corporación Regional de Desarrollo de Chuquisaca (Agreda et al. 1994).

La invasión del bosque por *Citrus* es inusual, ya que *Citrus* no se planta o dispersa por si sola en áreas donde ha sido introducida. Las semillas originales fueron llevadas al área probablemente por pastores atendiendo su ganado o por agricultores de subsistencia. Las frutas son comidas por animales como los joches (*Dasyprocta*), monos, y loros, y posiblemente también por ganado y tapires (dantas). La dispersion por gravedad puede también jugar un rol. Las áreas con los mayores grados de infestación por *Citrus* estuvieron en las cimas de las crestas y en los suelos húmedos de los valles, áreas donde el ganado pastorea más a menudo. En tales áreas, *Citrus* constituyo hasta el 45% de todos los árboles mayores de 10 cm de diámetro. La altitud parece ser un factor limitante, ya que *Citrus* no se encuentra cn áreas a mayor altura que 1900-2000 m. Aparentemente los Bosques Tucumano-Bolivianos en Bolivia no son los únicos bosques de ese tipo con la problemática de invasión de *Citrus*. *Citrus* es también una de las plantas exóticas más agresivas en el Bosque Tucumano-Boliviano del Parque Nacional El Rey en Salta, Argentina (Chalukian 1991).

La extracción de madera parece llevarse a cabo solo a menor escala, con la madera siendo sacada por mulas. Las especies maderables valiosas son *Juglans* y *Cedrela*. Las áreas más al sur, las que son accesibles por carretera, están siendo otorgadas en concesión por el gobierno a compañías privadas para operaciones futuras. Esto ha causado algunos temores en El Palmar, de que los bosques cercanos al pueblo que son usados por la comunidad local, puedan ser otorgados también a compañías foráneas.

En dos sobrevuelos separados (22 de mayo de 1995) hemos hecho un reconocimiento del paisaje de un área, inmediatamente al sur del Cerro Bufete, y hacia el norte hasta el Cerro Tigrecillos. Los claros en la vegetación pudieron ser vistos

throated Dipper) along the rivers that drain Cerro Bufete. This species previously was known only from extreme northern Argentina and from Tarija. It is confined to clear, fast streams and rivers; the extent of water pollution in northern Argentina has led to concern about this poorly-known, and apparently rare, bird.

The area around Cerro Bufete (2000 m) had an abundant and diverse small mammal fauna, including a montane rodent assemblage of at least seven species, and two marsupials, whereas at Limón (950 m) on the Río Santa Martha we collected only four rodents and one opossum. These differences in species richness are due to the difference in elevation between the sites; both sites likely have the same fauna at higher elevations. Bats were scarce at both sites, and we collected only eight species in all. At the Río Santa Martha there was evidence of a much greater abundance and diversity of larger mammals, especially in forests without cattle. The most prominent large mammal was the brown capuchin monkey (*Cebus apella*). Tracks of agoutis (*Dasyprocta*) were common at lower elevations, while tapirs (*Tapirus terrestris*) were abundant in higher, undisturbed forest, where there also was evidence of spectacled bears (*Tremarctos ornatus*). Along the Río Santa Martha, in the more inaccessible reaches near and above our camp at Limón, there were signs of a number of carnivores. However, both our observations and statements by our guides are in agreement that the region has relatively few species of large mammals.

The mammal fauna of this part of Bolivia is very poorly known, as evidenced by the fact that at least 10 of the species we encountered are not represented by any specimens from the Department of Chuquisaca, and at least half of the bats and marsupials collected (five species) are apparently new for the department.

The reptiles and amphibians of Chuquisaca were virtually unknown. Our survey recorded 32 species of reptiles and amphibians (16 species of frogs, 6 species of lizards, and 10 species of snakes). The herpetofauna of this region represents a mixture of Yungas species, species that invade the forest from the adjacent lowlands, and species of the Tucumano-Boliviano formation.

cerca a las partes bajas de todos los valles de ríos, y en las cuencas de los ríos Limonal y Cochayo se observaron algunos claros más arriba del valle. El valle del Río Santa Martha, más arriba del área donde tuvimos nuestro campamento en El Limón, no estaba visiblemente alterado. Es probable sin embargo que ahí haya ganado merodeando en las áreas más accesibles, especialmente en el lado sur del río. Vimos numerosos derrumbes en las laderas empinadas de esta cuenca.

Más de un cuarto de las especies de aves registradas en El Palmar y en las dos áreas de estudio no eran conocidas anteriormente, o fueron registradas recientemente para el departamento. Muchos de estos nuevos registros llenan los "huecos" en la distribución de las especies anteriormente conocidas de localidades tanto al norte (Santa Cruz) y al sur (Tarija o Argentina). Varias especies, como *Scytalopus bolivianus* (Southern White-crowned Tapaculo), *Mionectes striaticollis* (Streak-necked Flycatcher), *Chlorophonia cyanea* (Blue-naped Chlorophonia), *Anisognathus flavinucha* (Blue-winged Mountain-Tanager), y *Piranga leucoptera* (White-winged Tanager) que fueron encontrados durante el muestreo representan nuevos registros. Todas estas especies son típicas del bosque montano húmedo, y sugieren que los bosques cerca a El Palmar son más húmedos y más diversos que los bosques mejor conocidos de Tarija.

El descubrimiento ornitologico más importante fue el de una población de *Cinclus schulzi* (Rufous-throated Dipper) a lo largo de los ríos que desaguen el Cerro Bufete. Esta especie era conocida anteriormente sólo en el extremo norte de Argentina y de Tarija. Se encuentra limitada a riachuelos claros y rápidos y a ríos; el grado de polución del agua en el norte de Argentina ha despertado la preocupación sobre esta ave poco conocida y aparentemente rara.

El área en los alrededores del Cerro Bufete (2000 m) tuvo una abundante y diversa fauna de mamíferos pequeños, incluyendo a una composición de roedores montanos de por lo menos siete especies, y dos marsupiales, mientras que en Limón (950 m), en el Río Santa Martha hemos colectado solamente cuatro roedores y una zarigüeya. Esta diferencia en riqueza de especies es debida a diferencia en altitud entre los sitios; ambos lugares

El área en los alrededores del Cerro Bufete (2000 m) tuvo una abundante y diversa fauna de mamíferos pequeños.

Lowland species are Chacoan, with the exception of one Amazonian species. Diversity of the herpetofauna in the vicinity of El Palmar is quite low relative to that of the Yungas of Santa Cruz. Herpetofaunal diversity in this area may be the same as, or even higher than, that of the forests near Entre Rios, Tarija. Up to four taxa (two frogs, one snake, and one lizard) from this area may represent undescribed species.

CONSERVATION OPPORTUNITIES
(Bruce K. Holst, Thomas S. Schulenberg, and Louise H. Emmons)

In some respects the Bosque Tucumano-Boliviano is transitional between the more species-rich Yungas to the north, and drier forests to the south and east. The Tucumano-Boliviano region nonetheless constitutes a recognizable center of endemism. Furthermore, such forests in Bolivia are threatened if present trends of forest clearing are allowed to continue, yet currently receive little protection within Bolivia.

The areas north and west of El Palmar, in southern Chuquisaca, that were surveyed by the RAP team contain one of the largest remaining uninterrupted tracts of Bosque Tucumano-Boliviano remaining in Bolivia. Furthermore, we documented the presence in these forests of a high percentage of the endemic species that would be expected to occur. With no management efforts at all, some areas in this region, such as those on particularly steep or rocky slopes, will experience little or no disturbance for the foreseeable future. If habitat disturbance in the middle and lower portions of the Cochayo and Santa Martha river basins continues, however, then it is to be expected that the quality of all remaining forested areas, and watersheds, probably will face a continual decline. Therefore, these forests in southern Chuquisaca are worthy of efforts at protection.

There is little hunting in the areas that we visited. The principal threat to the biota of Tucumano-Boliviano forests in southern Bolivia is habitat disturbance and destruction. In the areas that we visited in south central Chuquisaca, such disturbance primarily took the form of cattle

probablamente tienen la misma fauna en las altitudes más altas. Los murciélagos fueron muy escasos en ambos sitios, y solamente hemos colectado ocho especies en total. En el Río Santa Martha encontramos evidencias de la presencia de una abundancia y diversidad de mamíferos más grandes mucho más alta, especialmente en los bosques sin presencia de ganado. El mamífero grande más notable era del mono capuchino marrón (*Cebus apella*). Las huellas de los joches (*Dasyprocta*) eran comunes en las elevaciones más bajas, mientras que las dantas (*Tapirus terrestris*) eran abundantes en los bosque más altos y sin tanta alteración donde también había evidencia de osos de anteojos (*Tremarctos ornatus*). A lo largo del Río Santa Martha, en los partes más inaccesibles cerca y más arriba de nuestro campamento en Limón, habían evidencias de varios carnívoros. Sin embargo, nuestras observaciones y los comentarios de nuestros guías están de acuerdo en que esta región tiene relativamente pocas especies de mamíferos grandes.

La fauna de mamíferos de este parte de Bolivia está muy poco conocida, tal como es evidenciado por el hecho que por lo menos 10 de las especies que hemos encontrado no están representadas por ninguno de los especímenes del Departamento de Chuquisaca, y que por lo menos la mitad de los murciélagos y los marsupiales colectados (cinco especies) son aparentemente especies nuevas para el departamento.

Los reptiles y anfibios de Chuquisaca eran casi desconocidos. Nuestro muestreo registro 32 especies de reptiles y anfibios (16 especies de ranas, 6 especies de lagartijas, y 10 especies de serpientes). La herpetofauna de esta región representa una mezcla de especies de los Yungas, de especies que invaden el bosque desde las zonas bajas adyacentes, y de especies de la formación Tucumano-Boliviana. Las especies de los zonas bajas son Chaqueñas, con la excepción de una especie Amazónica. La diversidad de herpetofauna en la vecindad de El Palmar es bastante baja en comparación a aquella de las Yungas de Santa Cruz. La diversidad de la herpetofauna en esta área puede ser la misma, o inclusive más alta, que las de los bosques cerca a Entre Ríos, Tarija. Hasta cuatro taxa (dos ranas, una serpiente, y una lagartija) de esta área pueden ser especies aún no descritas (es decir, especies nuevas).

The areas north and west of El Palmar that were surveyed contain one of the largest remaining uninterrupted tracts of Bosque Tucumano-Boliviano remaining in Bolivia.

grazing and the invasion of exotic *Citrus,* along with a small level of logging and farming.

The presence of cattle disturbs the forests in a number of ways, principally by changing the plant species composition of the understory, and preventing regeneration of all tree species whose seedlings they eat. Grazing by cattle may have changed the composition of the forests near El Palmar. Followup studies would need to be conducted in these forests to document the effects of grazing on tree recruitment and other demographic features. Burning also alters plant species composition, as does physical disturbance (trampling), which may open up areas for the invasion of exotic species.

The summit of Cerro Bufete, for example, is highly disturbed (although the species diversity of the steep slopes probably is protected, simply due to the ruggedness of the terrain). We recommend that Cerro Tigrecillos be included within any protected area that is established, as it forms a part of the Santa Martha basin and the vegetation on the summit remains in a natural state (and probably is similar to what the summit of Cerro Bufete used to look like).

Little can be done to control the invasion of *Citrus,* short of a monumental extraction effort similar to what is being done in Florida to remove *Melaleuca* and other exotics. This would be an extremely labor-intensive project, with no guarantee of success. *Citrus* seems to do well in areas that are disturbed, such as along ridges (which are disturbed by trails, cattle, and high winds) and in valley bottoms (disturbed by cattle and human occupation). Therefore, the invasive species of *Citrus* now found in the forests in the valley and along the ridge-tops must be considered to be established. Despite the presence of this exotic species, many elements of the native biota still are present. *Citrus* also is absent from areas that are cattle-free, and colonization in higher elevations (above about 1700 m) will be inhibited by colder temperatures.

The small scale logging that we saw currently has a minimal impact, particularly since there are no roads into the region and timber must be carried out on animals. Commercial logging, on the other hand, would result in massive disturbance

OPORTUNIDADES PARA LA CONSERVACIÓN
(Bruce K. Holst, Thomas S. Schulenberg, y Louise H. Emmons)

En algunos aspectos el bosque Tucumano-Boliviano es transicional entre las Yungas más rica en especies hacia el norte, y los bosques más secos hacia el sur y el este. De todas formas, la región Tucumano-Boliviana constituye un centro de endemismo reconocible. Más aun, tales bosques en Bolivia están amenazados si es que las tendencias actuales de corte del bosque son permitidas de continuar y actualmente estos reciben poca protección en Bolivia.

Las áreas al norte y oeste de El Palmar, en el sur de Chuquisaca, que fueron muestreadas por el equipo del RAP contienen uno de los últimos trechos de bosques ininterrumpidos de bosques Tucumano-Boliviano que quedan en Bolivia. Más aun, hemos documentado la presencia en estos bosques de un alto porcentaje de especies endémicas que se esperarían hallar. Sin ningún tipo de manejo, algunas áreas de esta región, como aquellas en laderas empinadas o rocosas, sufrirán poco o ninguna perturbación en el futuro previsible. Si continua la perturbación del hábitat en las porciones intermedias y bajas de las cuencas de los ríos Cochayo y Santa Martha, se esperaría sin embargo que la calidad de todas las áreas boscosas que quedan, y de las cuencas, probablemente enfrentarán una degradación continúa. Por lo tanto, estos bosques en el sur de Chuquisaca merecen la aplicación de medidas de protección.

Hay poca cacería en las áreas que hemos visitado. La principal amenaza para la biota de los bosques Tucumano-Bolivianos en el sur de Bolivia es la perturbación y destrucción de hábitats. En las áreas que hemos visitado en el sur central de Chuquisaca, tales perturbaciones tomaron principalmente la forma de ganadería y de la invasión de un *Citrus* exótico, junto con un grado bajo de tala de madera y agricultura.

La presencia de ganado perturba el bosque en varias formas, principalmente al cambiar la composición de las especies de plantas del soto-bosque, previniendo la regeneración de todas las especies de árboles cuyas semillas son comidas

Las áreas al norte y oeste de El Palmar que fueron muestreadas el contienen uno de los últimos trechos de bosques ininterrumpidos de bosques Tucumano-Boliviano que quedan en Bolivia.

that would provide additional habitat for the invasion of *Citrus* trees into the forest at the lower elevations; would increase erosion; provide roads that would allow humans, and their cattle, to move deeper into the area; and could take away the local, small-scale, probably somewhat sustainable logging we observed and heard about. In addition, it could deplete some of the endemics or near endemics tree species currently found in the region. Preserving adequate habitat for regenerating valuable timber trees also should be an important consideration for the local residents.

The middle and upper portions of the basins of the ríos Cochayo and Santa Martha (above ca. 1500 m) in particular are largely intact and could serve as the 'nucleus' for a protected area. Although we did not enter the basin of the Río Nuevo, just to the south of Cerro Bufete, this forest looks to be of similar composition, and to be relatively free of human disturbance. We recommend additional surveys of this, and similar, areas to establish their suitability for incorporation into such a protected area.

The lower Cochayo and Santa Martha basins, although retaining some forest, in contrast are much more heavily disturbed. These also are the areas that are subject to the greatest level of exploitation by local communities. Therefore, even if, as we recommend, strict controls on logging and agriculture are placed on forests in the upper portions of these basins, it should be possible to develop management plans that would allow for sustainable uses of the lower-elevation forests that currently are relied upon by local communities. Such a prospect would specifically preclude commercial logging from this area. Perhaps a small forestry station could be established to investigate extraction rates that would allow these zones to be utilized on a sustainable basis (i.e., that does not permit further environmental degradation).

por ellos. El pastoreo del ganado puede haber cambiado la composición de los bosques cerca a El Palmar. Se necesitarían llevara a cabo estudios de seguimiento para documentar los efectos del pastoreo sobre la regeneración natural de los árboles y de otras variables demograficas. La quema también altera la composición de las especies de plantas, así como también las perturbaciones físicas (compactación), lo cual puede abrir áreas para la invasión de especies exóticas.

La cumbre del Cerro Bufete está, por ejemplo, altamente perturbada (aunque la diversidad de especies de las laderas está probablemente protegida simplemente debido a la dificultad del terreno). Recomendamos que el Cerro Tigrecillos sea incluido dentro de cualquier tipo de área protegida que sea establecida, dado que este forma parte de la cuenca del Santa Martha y que la vegetación del la cima aún se encuentra en un estado natural (y probablemente es similar a lo que alguna vez fue la cima del Cerro Bufete).

Poco se puede hacer para controlar la invasión de *Citrus*, tanto como el esfuerzo monumental que se está haciendo en Florida para erradicar *Malaleuca* y otras especies exóticas. Esto sería un proyecto extremadamente trabajoso y sin garantía de éxito. *Citrus* parece favorecerse en áreas perturbadas, tales como a lo largo de las crestas, (que están perturbadas por el ganado, trochas, y fuerte viento), en los fondos de los valles (perturbados por el ganado y la ocupación humana). Por lo tanto, las especies invasoras de *Citrus* encontradas ahora en los bosques en el valle y a lo largo de las partes altas de las crestas, deben ser consideradas como ya establecidas. A pesar de la presencia de especies exóticas, muchas elementos de la biota nativa están aún presentes. *Citrus* está también ausente en las áreas donde no hay ganadería, y su colonización en las áreas a altitudes mayores (sobre los 1700 m) será inhibida por la baja temperatura.

La extracción de madera que vimos tiene actualmente un mínimo impacto, particularmente porque ahí no hay pistas que entren a la región y la madera tiene que ser sacada con animales. Por otro lado, la tala comercial resultaría en una perturbación masiva que proporcionaría hábitats adicionales para la invasión de árboles de *Citrus* en el bosque a elevaciones menores; incrementaría la erosión; proveería con las pistas que permitirían a los humanos, y su ganado, a penetrar más adentro en el área; y terminaría con la tala a menor escala, quizá algo sostenible que hemos observado y de la que hemos escuchado. Adicionalmente, esta podría acabar con algunos de las especies de árboles endémicas o casi endémicas actualmente halladas en la región. La preservación del hábitat adecuado para la regeneración de las especies maderables valiosas también debería ser una consideración importante para los residentes locales.

Las porciones medias y altas de las cuencas de los ríos Cochayo y Santa Martha en particular (sobre ca. 1500 m) están en gran parte intactas y podrían servir como el "núcleo" para un área protegida. Aunque no hemos entrado a la cuenca del Río Nuevo, inmediatamente al sur del Cerro Bufete, ese bosque parece tener una composición similar y estar desprovisto de perturbaciones humanas. Recomendamos reconocimientos adicionales de esta, o de otras áreas similares, para establecer que tan apropiadas puedan ser para incorporarlas en el área protegida.

En contraste, las cuencas bajas del Cochayo y Santa Martha, aunque contienen algo de bosque, están perturbadas mucho más severamente. Estas son también las áreas que están sujetas al grado más alto de explotación por las comunidades locales. Por lo tanto, aunque, tal como lo recomendamos, se apliquen controles estrictos para la tala y agricultura en los bosques de las porciones altas de las cuencas, debería ser posible desarrollar planes de manejo que pemitirian la explotación para usos sostenibles de los bosques a menor altura que son de las que actualmente dependen las comunidades locales. Tal plan excluiría específicamente a los extractores de madera comerciales de esta área. Quizá, se podría establecer una estación forestal pequeña para investigar las tasas de extracción que podría permitir un uso sostenible a esta zona (es decir, que no permita una mayor degradación ambiental).

Las porciones medias y altas de las cuencas de los ríos Cochayo y Santa Martha podrían servir como el "núcleo" para un área protegida.

RAP sites from the
1995 expedition.
See also gazeteer,
page 40.

64°27'W
20°30'S

Rio Pejes

Timbo
Tigrecillos

Rio Pilcomayo

BOLIVIA

Río Santa Martha
Cerro Tigrecillos
Rio Urucuti
Limon
Rio Cochayo

CHUQUISACA

La Mesada
Rio Limonal   El Ajial

La Quebrada
Ovejerias
Bufete
El Palmar   Juntas de
Aracubi   Cambari
Aracubi

Abras de Arenal
Arenal
Rio Nuevo   Ipirenda

Rio
Pilcomayo

Rio Nuevo
Limon

Rio San Simon
Candado
Chico

Cerro Bravo
Manzanal
Rio Manzanal

Rio Pilaya

Candado
Grande

Rio Pilaya
Huasurenda
Cañon Verde

21°09'S
64°08'W

LEGEND

*   RAP sites

•   Pueblos

↗   Airstrip

─   Rios

━   Limite Cantonal

TECHNICAL REPORT

VEGETATION OF TUCUMANO-BOLI-VIANO FORESTS IN CHUQUISACA, BOLIVIA (Bruce Holst)

Tucumano-Boliviano forests in the broad sense can be summarized as follows: semideciduous to semievergreen, middle montane cloudforests with a predominance of Myrtaceae and Lauraceae. They are strongly influenced by the cool to cold temperatures in the winter, relatively high moisture levels (from both fog and rain), and steep topography. Tucumano-Boliviano forests begin in the north near the latitude of the city of Santa Cruz in the Bolivian departments of Santa Cruz and southern Cochabamba, where they are transitional with more tropical, moist montane forests. Southward, they continue into the departments of Chuquisaca and Tarija departments, and then in an interrupted line south into Argentina in Salta, Jujuy, Tucumán and northern Catamarca Provinces. They are the southernmost subset of Yungas forests, the moist, montane forests forming a near continuous band along the eastern Andes from Venezuela to northern Argentina. In Chuquisaca, we found the majority of these forests on irregular, steep mountains with deep canyons and narrow ridges. The two exceptions to this topography in the area we visited were Cerro Bufete and Cerro Tigrecillos, two mountains with relatively flat summits and with at least a portion of their walls containing vertical drops of several hundred meters.

While Tucumano-Boliviano forests are rela-
tively well-studied in Argentina (Brown et al. 1985, Cabrera 1956, 1976, Grau 1985, Grau and Brown 1995, Moyano and Movia 1989), rather little is known about their composition and full extension in Bolivia. An unpublished report from the department of Tarija was prepared by James Solomon of the Missouri Botanical Garden, and some studies by the Departamento de Recursos Naturales of Chuquisaca have been made. We were able to sample Tucumano-Boliviano forests in two main areas in central-south Chuquisaca Department: the forests surrounding Cerro Bufete just west of El Palmar; and the slopes and summit of Cerro Los Tigrecillos on the northern side of the Río Santa Martha valley.

The forests that we studied compared very well in composition with those reported from Argentina at a similar elevation (Brown et al. 1985). Overall, Tucumano-Boliviano forests have a strong presence of Myrtaceae, with five important genera: *Myrcianthes, Siphoneugena, Blepharocalyx, Myrcia* and *Myrciaria*. *Siphoneugena occidentalis* and *Myrcianthes pseudomato* are perhaps the most characteristic species in Tucumano-Boliviano forests, and they fairly well define Tucumano-Boliviano forest distribution except for a disjunct population of *S. occidentalis* in Mato Grosso, Brazil. Other important families that also share species between the Tucumano-Boliviano forests in Bolivia and Argentina are: Lauraceae (*Phoebe porphyria*), Mimosaceae (*Anadenanthera macrocarpa, Parapiptadenia excelsa, Enterolobium contor-*

tisiliquum), Fabaceae (*Myroxylon peruiferum, Tipuana tipu*), Piperaceae (*Piper tucumanum*), Sapindaceae (*Allophyllus edulis*), Combretaceae (*Terminalia triflora*), and Meliaceae (*Cedrela lilloi*).

A few species very common in the Argentinian Tucumano-Boliviano forests were represented in the Bolivian ones by only a few individuals, such as *Pisonia ambigua* (Nyctaginaceae), *Urera baccifera* (Urticaceae), *Vassobia breviflora* (Solanaceae), or were not found in the Bolivian forests: *Achatocarpus* sp. and *Bouganvillea stipitata* (Nyctaginaceae), and *Patagonula americana* (Boraginaceae). These species may be found at drier or lower altitudes in Bolivia where we did not run any transects. Palms were completely absent in the Tucumano-Boliviano forests we visited, as well as in those in Argentina.

Economically or compositionally important endemic, or near endemic, tree species of Tucumano-Boliviano forests include *Ilex argentina* (Aquifoliaceae), *Tabebuia lapacho* (Bignoniaceae), *Viburnum seemenii* (Caprifoliaceae), *Terminalia triflora* (Combretaceae), *Agarista boliviensis* (Ericaceae), *Crinodendron tucumanum* (Elaeocarpaceae), *Lonchocarpus lilloi* and *Tipuana tipu* (Fabaceae), *Juglans australis* (Juglandaceae), *Nectandra angusta* and *Phoebe porphyria* (Lauraceae), *Inga saltensis* (Mimosaceae), *Amomyrtella guili, Myrcianthes callicoma,* and *Myrcianthes pseudomato* (Myrtaceae), *Podocarpus parlatorei* (Podocarpaceae), *Prunus tucumanensis* (Rosaceae), and *Aegiphila saltensis* (Verbenaceae). An additional tree species, *Cedrela lilloi* (Meliaceae), is not restricted to Tucumano-Boliviano forests but occurs there in stands of economic—and conservation—importance.

We were unable to reach the higher altitude (2500-3000 m elevation) forests that were reported by Fjeldså and Mayer (1996) to have large stands of *Podocarpus parlatorei* and *Alnus acuminata*. Additional botanical studies in those areas, as well as the upper reaches of the Cochayo and Santa Martha river basins and forests south-southwest of Cerro Bufete in the Río Nuevo basin are needed to provide a more complete picture of the extent and composition of Tucumano-Boliviano forests in Sud Cinti Province of Chuquisaca Department.

Methods

We made 11 Rapid Transects at elevations between 900 and 2200 m (Appendix 2). General collections of fertile plants were made whenever possible, including areas outside of the transect lines but at comparable elevations, as well as at slightly higher elevations (Appendix 1). In conducting the transects (following the methods of Foster 1993), a measuring line was carried through a single habitat type; as the line was reeled out, all trees > 10 cm dbh that fell within a 5 m wide path on either side of the line were identified, and collected as necessary. After 100 trees were counted, the distance of the transect line was measured. We also collected and took further notes on abundance and density of understory trees. Trees > 10 cm dbh were divided into two size classes, trees 10-30 cm dbh and trees > 30 cm dbh. Herbarium collections were made of all species encountered, and recollecting was done if there was any doubt as to the identity if a taxon or if better material was found.

Collections

Including the vouchers for the transects, we made 707 collections of plants, the majority of these with three to five duplicates. The first set was deposited at the herbarium of the Museo de Historia Natural Noel Kempff in Santa Cruz (SCZ), and the second set at the Field Museum of Natural History in Chicago (F). Additional sets are to be distributed from SCZ.

Climate

The rainy season usually occurs between October and April. Total annual precipitation in the region is approximately 1,200 mm/year and is the wettest known portion of southern Bolivia. The annual average temperature is ca. 21°C, but according to our informants, freezing temperatures are not uncommon and there has been snowfall even as low as El Palmar (1100 m elevation).

Cedrela lilloi occurs in stands of economic—and conservation— importance.

Soils

Soils are relatively shallow and rock outcrops are frequent. Due to the steep topography and relatively unstable soils, landslides are very common on many hillsides, which would help account for the higher species diversity that we counted on slopes. Cerro Bufete stands out in the region because of its mesa-like appearance, and being largely sandstone with acidic soils, has a distinct flora for its corresponding elevation. Aluminum is reported to occur at toxic levels, the soils are neutral to acidic in pH, and the fertility is low to moderate.

Site Descriptions

The expedition was divided up into three main study areas: the slopes and summit of Cerro Bufete, the middle Río Santa Martha valley, and slopes and summits of Cerro Tigrecillos. The highest altitudes were reached on Cerro Bufete (2580 m) and Cerro Tigrecillos (2150 m). All of the area studied lies in the Río Urucuti drainage, which generally flows from west to east. The Urucuti is a tributary of the Río Pilcomayo, which in turn is a major tributary of the Paraná and then of the Río de la Plata.

Cerro Bufete

Slopes
From the drier, mostly deciduous forests that border El Palmar at about 1100 m elevation, the mountains to the west rise steeply. The additional moisture intercepted from winds, the cold weather, and fog during the strong dry season combine to produce a semideciduous to semievergreen cloud forest on upper slopes and deep canyons.

Between 1300 and 1600 m, the forests were tall (20-30 m), semideciduous, and with a relatively high number of epiphytic bryophytes and pteridophytes. Deciduous trees were *Tabebuia lapacho* (Bignoniaceae), *Crinodendron tucumanum* (Elaeocarpaceae), *Prunus tucumanum* (Rosaceae), *Parapiptadenia excelsa* (Mimosaceae), and evergreen trees, mostly *Siphoneugena occidentalis* (Myrtaceae), *Ocotea* and *Persea* (Lauraceae), *Chrysophyllum gono-*

carpum (Sapotaceae), *Pogonopus tubulosus* (Rubiaceae) and *Cupania vernalis* (Sapindaceae). Herbaceous plants include many ferns such as *Asplenium pumulum, Adiantum raddianum, Adiantopsis radiata,* and *Pteridium arachnoideum,* as well as *Ruellia sanguinea* (Acanthaceae), *Piper tucumanum* (Piperaceae), and shrubs and small trees were *Miconia calvescens* (Melastomataceae), *Luehea fiebrigii* (Tiliaceae), *Bocconia pearcei* (Papaveraceae), *Solanum schlechtendalianum* (Solanaceae), and *Senna hirsuta* (Caesalpiniaceae).

The most noticeable change in vegetation occurs at about 1500 m elevation, where the most characteristic species of these forests, *Siphoneugena occidentalis* (Myrtaceae), begins to appear, and where epiphyte abundance and diversity markedly increase.

The taller (20-30 m) forests of the slopes and valley bottoms in this area (1500-2000 m elevation; Appendix 2, Transect 2) usually were dominated by *Siphoneugena occidentalis* (Myrtaceae), but also had Lauraceae, *Blepharocalyx salicifolius* (Myrtaceae), *Parapiptadenia* sp. (Mimosaceae), *Tabebuia lapacho* (Bignoniaceae), *Crinodendron tucumanum* (Elaeocarpaceae), and scattered *Cedrela lilloi* (Meliaceae) and *Juglans australis* (Juglandaceae). These forests had an irregular canopy, with widely scattered emergent trees (*Crinondendron tucumanum, Cedrela lilloi*), and dense pockets of 3-7 m tall tree ferns (*Alsophila incana*). A very common shrub throughout this area was cf. *Brunfelsia australis* (Solanaceae), accounting for up to 1/3 of the individual shrubs. Other common shrubs were *Psychotria yungasensis* (Rubiaceae), *Jungia pauciflora* (Asteraceae), *Solanum* spp. (Solanaceae), *Boehmeria caudata* (Urticaceae), and *Diplazium lilloi* (Pteridophyta). Epiphytes were abundant, particularly the long-pendent moss *Pilotrichella pentasticha*, which gave this forest its characteristic appearance. Other epiphytes were *Rhipsalis tucumanensis* (Cactaceae), *Peperomia tominiana* (Piperaceae), *Elaphoglossum* sp., *Huperzia* aff. *hartwegiana, Microgramma squamulosa, Pecluma eurybasis* var. *glabrescens* and *Polypodium latipes* (Pteridophyta) as well as another, possibly undescribed species of *Polypodium* (A. R. Smith, pers. com.).

The most noticeable change in vegetation occurs at about 1500 m elevation.

Understory herbs were dominated by ferns, including *Asplenium* vel aff. *argentinum, A. serra, A. rigidum, Blechnum sprucei, Polypodium latipes, Pteris deflexa,* and *Thelypteris* cf. *jujuyensis.* The understory also contained *Hydrocotyle humboldtii* (Apiaceae), *Tradescantia* sp. (Commelinaceae), *Rhynchospora* sp. (Cyperaceae), *Panicum* sp. (Poaceae), and *Peperomia blanda* (Piperaceae).

Abundant tree ferns (*Alsophila incana*) and drooping mosses seemed to mark the wettest areas of the forests. These wet forests occurred in the two places where we climbed up the mountains, both at about 1900 to 2000 meters elevation, but probably form a band all along the mountain range where there is ample rainfall along with a higher degree of fog during the dry season.

On the drier, western side of the ridge, a more gently sloping forest with many large diameter trees occurs (Appendix 2, Transect 4). These drier forests share many species in common with the *Siphoneugena-Alsophila* forest on the eastern side of the same hill, but have *Myrcianthes pseudomato, Myrcia* cf. *multiflora,* and *Blepharocalyx salicifolius* (all Myrtaceae) as the three most common species, and no *Siphoneugena* were encountered at all. *Myrcianthes pseudomato* is endemic to Tucumano-Boliviano forests. Other canopy trees were *Viburnum seemenii* (Caprifoliaceae), *Prunus tucumanensis* (Rosaceae), *Persea* sp. (Lauraceae), and *Oreopanax* cf. *boliviensis* (Araliaceae). This forest had the most trees > 30 cm dbh of any that we surveyed (24/100 individuals). Emergent trees, to ca. 35 m tall, were *Blepharocalyx salicifolius* (Myrtaceae), *Parapiptadenia excelsa* (Mimosaceae), and *Cedrela lilloi* (Meliaceae), and understory trees included *Allophyllus edulis* (Sapindaceae), *Aegiphila saltensis* and *Duranta serratifolia* (both Verbenaceae). Just outside the border of our transect we observed several individuals of emergent *Juglans australis* (Juglandaceae). As with the *Siphoneugena-Alsophila* forest, the dominant shrub was cf. *Brunfelsia australis* (Solanaceae), along with smaller individuals of *Myrcia* cf. *multiflora, Solanum* aff. *glaucophyllum* (Solanaceae), *Dicliptera tweediana* (Acanthaceae), and *Chusquea* sp. (Poaceae). Common herbs were

Pteris deflexa and *Polystichum nudicaule* (both Pteridophyta), *Psychotria yungasensis* (Rubiaceae), *Dicliptera* aff. *tweediana* (Acanthaceae), *Hydrocotyle humboldtii* (Apiaceae), *Panicum* sp. (Poaceae), *Tradescantia* sp. (Commelinaceae), *Rhynchospora* sp. (Cyperaceae), and *Asplenium* vel aff. *argentinum* (Pteridophyta).

As in many other areas of the region as seen by air, the steep slopes of the Río Limonal canyon north of Cerro Bufete had numerous landslides in differing stages of succession. We were unable to visit any very recent landslides, but several older ones contained concentrated stands of a single species, *Aegiphila saltensis* (Verbenaceae). Besides the patches of *Aegiphila,* which were about 15 m tall, the forest in this area was 20-25 m tall, and had *Allophyllus edulis* and *Cupania vernalis* (both Sapindaceae), *Phoebe porphyria* (Lauraceae), *Ilex argentina* (Aquifoliaceae), *Croton quadrisetosus* (Euphorbiaceae), *Roupala meisneri* (Proteaceae), and *Myrcianthes* spp. (Myrtaceae). A common emergent tree that we were unable to collect (perhaps *Crinodendron tucumanun,* Elaeocarpaceae) was found towards the bottom of the slope, perhaps spared by the landslide. Slightly more open areas on the landslide were densely covered with *Celtis iguanaea* (Ulmaceae), *Rubus boliviensis* (Rosaceae), and contained occasional *Dodonea viscosa* (Sapindaceae). Common herbs were *Iresine diffusa* (Amaranthaceae), *Dicliptera* aff. *tweediana* (Acanthaceae), and *Psychotria yungasensis* (Rubiaceae).

The beds of most of the rivers in the region are narrow, rocky channels. The Río Limonal near the base of Cerro Bufete is strewn with large boulders. Dense mats of bryophytes and pteridophytes (*Lellingeria obovata, Elaphoglossum piloselloides, Selaginella novae-hollandiae*) grew in the spray from the numerous small to high waterfalls, and dense herbaceous cover including the showy *Fuchsia boliviana* (Onagraceae) grew on the steep walls of the lower part of Cerro Bufete. Just above the exposed rocky part of the river on very steep slopes, a belt of shrubs and small trees occurred, including *Alnus acuminata* (Betulaceae), *Amomyrtella guili* (Myrtaceae), *Schinus myrtifolius* (Anacardiaceae), *Duranta serratifolia* (Verbenaceae), *Phenax laevigatus* (Urticaceae), as

*Abundant tree ferns (*Alsophila incana*) and drooping mosses mark the wettest areas of the forests.*

well as scattered small trees of *Phoebe porphyria* (Lauraceae) and *Cupania vernalis* (Sapindaceae). Herbaceous plants right along the river among the boulders were *Psychotria yungasensis* (Rubiaceae), *Piper hieronymi* (Piperaceae), and *Boehmeria caudata* (Urticaceae).

Ridge tops between 1800 and 2200 m elevation, and plateaus that we visited to the north and northwest of Cerro Bufete, and portions of the summit of Cerro Tigrecillos (Appendix 2, Transects 1, 8, 9), had low (5-15 m tall) forests composed mainly of *Ilex argentina* (Aquifoliaceae), *Viburnum seemenii* (Caprifoliaceae), *Clethra scabra* (Clethraceae), *Prunus tucumanensis* (Rosaceae), *Myrsine coriacea* (Myrsinaceae), *Roupala meisneri* (Proteaceae) and *Symplocos* aff. *subcuneata* (Symplocaceae). The density of stems was among the highest that we sampled, and no trees measured greater than 30 cm dbh. Species diversity was among the lowest we encountered, with only 12 species counted out of 100 individuals, with the bulk of the individuals accounted for by the first three species listed above. There were very few vascular epiphytes in these forests, and the understory was mostly open, perhaps partially due to the higher presence of cattle in these more accessible areas. Shrubs or small trees (< 10 cm dbh) were *Myrsine coriacea*, *Myrcia* cf. *multiflora*, and *Roupala meisneri*. Common herbs were an unidentified species of *Panicum* (Poaceae), *Hydrocotyle humboldtii* (Apiaceae), *Polystichum nudicaule* and *Blechnum glandulosum* (Pteridophyta), and *Psychotria yungasensis* (Rubiaceae).

Walls

The steep slopes of Cerro Bufete are inaccessible in most areas of the north, east and south sides of the mountain, but a single, long-used, steep trail leading up from the lowlands in the north offers a cross section through several dramatically different vegetation types. The trail is very rocky from base to summit and cattle graze along its path and accessible areas off of it. Some evidence of fire was evident, but the large expanses of rock offer some protection to the vegetation. The lower, tall, moist forests that surround the base of the wall extend upwards in the few steep canyons. In these moist or wet areas, large boulders were conspicu-

ously dotted with huge individuals of a Bromeliaceae species (probably *Tillandsia australis*) that we could not collect, and with a clumping species of *Lamprothyrsus* (Poaceae) with long, pendent leaves. Above these moist lower slopes, or on steep ridges, isolated patches of mostly evergreen shrub forest were found among areas with large boulders. Common species in these areas were *Schinus myrtifolius* (Anacardiaceae), *Viburnum seemenii* (Caprifoliaceae), *Columellia oblonga* (Columelliaceae), *Myrsine coriacea* (Myrsinaceae), *Amomyrtella guili* (Myrtaceae), *Monnina conferta* (Polygalaceae), *Escallonia hypoglauca* (Saxifragaceae), *Symplocos* aff. *subcuneata* (Symplocaceae), *Chusquea* sp. (Poaceae), and had an occasional columnar cactus growing directly on top of the boulders. Above the shrub belt, on more exposed slopes with smaller rocks or on vertical walls, the vegetation was lower and contained a complex mixture of herbaceous or suffruticose species. Two species of Bromeliaceae (probably *Puya*) were very common in this area and formed conspicuous gray clumps easily visible from a distance. Other common species were *Eryngium elegans* (Apiaceae), *Achyrocline latifolia*, *Chromolaena connivens* and *Eupatorium bupleurifolium* (Asteraceae), *Collaea speciosa* (Fabaceae), *Hypericum silenoides* (Clusiaceae), *Gentianella* spp. (Gentianaceae), *Axonopus compressus* and *Schizacaryum microstachyum* (Poaceae), and *Agalinus genistifolia* (Scrophulariaceae). The lithophytic vegetation (that found on steep, rocky walls) in this area included *Sisyrinchium alatum* (Iridaceae), *Oxalis mollissima* (Oxalidaceae), *Anemia ferruginea* var. *ferruginea*, *Elaphoglossum cuspidatum* and *Lycopodium thyoides* (Pteridophyta), and *Peperomia silvarum* (Piperaceae). *Drosera villosa* (Droseraceae) formed small colonies on muddy banks near the summit among shrublets of *Gaultheria vaccinioides* (Ericaceae) and several pteridophyte species.

Summit

Cerro Bufete is a high, plateau-like mesa with most of its summit at approximately 2300 m elevation with a prominent dome reaching nearly 2600 m. Cerro Bufete has nearly vertical walls on the east, a ridge connecting it to the higher reaches of the Andes to the west, and steeply sloping hills on the north and south. Much of the summit forms the headwaters of the Río Limonal, which falls off the northern scarp in a beautiful waterfall. Large portions of the summit currently are covered by pasture, which is maintained by occasional burning. Dwarf forest remains along streams and on steep, rocky slopes.

Gallery forests on the table-top portion of the summit range from 5 to 10 m tall, were dominated by *Crinodendron tucumanum* (Elaeocarpaceae), and had a high abundance of epiphytic bryophytes, lichens, pteridophytes, and *Senecio epiphyticus* (Asteraceae). The gray color of the numerous lichens gives the forest a characteristic color after the trees have shed their leaves. *Alnus acuminata* (Betulaceae) and *Croton* sp. (Euphorbiaceae) also were common trees in this forest, which contains scattered individuals of *Podocarpus parlatorei* (Podocarpaceae). Understory shrubs were comprised mostly of *Aequatorium repandum* (Asteraceae), *Bejaria aestuans* (Ericaceae), and *Escallonia hypoglauca* (Saxifragaceae).

The dwarf forests that occur on steep or protected areas had *Symplocos* aff. *subcuneata* (Symplocaceae), *Ilex argentina* (Aquifoliaceae), *Viburnum seemenii* (Caprifoliaceae), and *Berberis fiebrigii* (Berberidaceae). Open areas were dominated by grasses (principally *Agrostis*?*)* and sedges and contain many species of Asteraceae. The streams, particularly where the trail crosses, were heavily eroded by the cattle, and additional larger scale erosion can be seen in some of the pasture areas.

The trail leading along the ridge west of Cerro Bufete (ca. 2500 m elevation) had evidence of fire and our guide told us that several years prior to our visit, a large fire burned most of the slopes leading up to the ridge. There was much evidence of cattle and semi-wild mules were seen. The open areas had a similar herbaceous component as that of Cerro Bufete. The forest remnants were low in this area and consisted of scattered *Alnus acuminata* (Betulaceae), *Polylepis hieronymi* (Rosaceae), and *Podocarpus parlatorei* (Podocarpaceae), with occasional patches of

dense shrubs including *Baccharis chilco* and *B. dracunculifolia* (Asteraceae), *Berberis fiebrigii* (Berberidaceae), *Columellia oblonga* (Columelliaceae), *Mimosa lepidota* (Mimosaceae), and *Myrica pubescens* (Myriacaceae). The rich herbaceous component was dominated by Asteraceae (including *Ageratina azangaroensis, A. tenuis, Antennaria linearifolia, Bidens andicola, Ophyrosporus kuntzei, Stevia calderillensis, S. fruticosa,* and *S. grisebachiana*), as well as *Eryngium elegans* (Apiaceae), *Calamagrostis* sp. (Poaceae), and *Geranium* aff. *fallax* (Geraniaceae).

The *pajonales* or pastures were composed mostly of Poaceae, but had scattered herbs such as *Gentianella silenoides* (Gentianaceae), *Cuphea calophylla* (Lythraceae), *Bidens pilosa* (Asteraceae), and the subshrub *Senecio clivicolus* (Asteraceae). Rocky savannas had *Geranium pflanzii* (Geraniaceae), *Euphorbia portulacoides* (Euphorbiaceae), and *Lupinus celsimontanus* (Fabaceae), and patches of *Drosera villosa* (Droseraceae) were locally common among the grasses.

Río Santa Martha

Valley
The Río Santa Martha valley is one of the least disturbed in the region, at least in regard to deforestation. Though we were unable to enter the higher reaches of the canyon due to the steep slopes, from the point where we entered the valley near its confluence with the Río Urucuti, and as evidenced from overflights, we saw no permanent habitations nor clearings. Cattle are grazed in the forest along the lower stretches of the valley and at least on the northern ridge. The valley bottom at about 900 m elevation was fairly moist and supports a heavier epiphytic Angiosperm flora than any other place we visited. *Vriesea maxoniana* (Bromeliaceae) was very common as well as several species of *Peperomia* and ferns. Lianas also were very common in this forest, including Hippocrateaceae, Bignoniaceae, and Sapindaceae. The understory was open, probably the result of long-term cattle grazing, but a few dominant herbs are probably unpalatable to the livestock, particularly *Psychotria yungasensis* (Rubiaceae) and *Lastreopsis effusa* (Pteridophyta).

The gray color of the numerous lichens gives the forest a characteristic color after the trees have shed their leaves.

Some herbaceous vegetation grew among the rocks along the river such as *Equisetum bogotense* (Pteridophyta), *Cuphea racemosa* (Lythraceae), *Blechnum lanceola* (Pteridophyta), and *Polygonum punctatum* (Polygonaceae), and in the sand along the bank, *Cyperus laxus* (Cyperaceae), *Ichnanthus tenuis* and *Paspalum mandiocum* (Poaceae), *Asplenium* sp. (Pteridophyta), and *Boehmeria cylindrica* (Urticaceae).

Trees along the river included *Juglans australis* (Juglandaceae), *Cedrela lilloi* (Meliaceae), *Siphoneugena occidentalis* (Myrtaceae), *Ficus guarantica* (Moraceae), *Nectandra angusta* (Lauraceae), and *Chrysophyllum gonocarpum* (Sapotaceae). A small tree with old fruits found along the river is likely *Calycorectes psidiiflorus* (Myrtaceae), which would be a new record for the country.

Above the steep banks, on the high terrace, a tall forest with a dense herbaceous undercover of *Lastreopsis effusa* (Pteridophyta) occurs and contains numerous lianas (Appendix 2, Transect 5). This forest had the highest incidence of *Citrus* invasion of any we had seen, with 45 of 100 trees (> 10 cm dbh) being *Citrus aurantium* (Rutaceae). This forest also had many species not found elsewhere by us such as *Piper tucumanum* (Piperaceae), *Nectandra angusta* (Lauraceae), *Inga marginata* (Mimosaceae), *Citronella apogon* (Icacinaceae), *Lonchocarpus lilloi* (Fabaceae), *Enterolobium contortisiliquum* (Mimosaceae), *Pisonia ambigua* (Nyctaginaceae), *Maclura tinctoria* (Moraceae), and *Turpinia* cf. *occidentalis* (Staphyleaceae).

Northern Ridge

Ascending above the flood plain, the steep rocky slopes support a rather dry and much shorter forest (5-15 m) than the valley bottom or ridge tops.

The hilltop immediately to the north of Río Santa Martha at about 1000 to 1100 m elevation (Appendix 2, Transect 6) had a tall mixed forest dominated by *Siphoneugena occidentalis* and *Myrciaria* cf. *floribunda* (Myrtaceae), and *Prunus integrifolia* (Rosaceae). Other common trees were *Tabebuia* cf. *chrysantha* (Bignoniaceae), *Roupala montana* (Proteaceae), and *Clethra* spp. (Clethraceae). There were numerous lianas pre-

sent and the shrubby understory was quite dense. The herbaceous layer was dominated by *Asplenium* vel aff. *argentinum* (Pteridophyta) and *Olyra fasciculata* (Poaceae). Just above this area we saw some of the largest trees in the forest, *Juglans australis* (Juglandaceae).

A slightly higher elevation forest at 1300 m elevation along the same ridge was the most diverse we encountered on the trip with 24 species out of the 100 trees > 10 cm dbh. *Siphoneugena occidentalis* (Myrtaceae) was the most common canopy tree, but the small understory tree *Trichilia clausseni* (Meliaceae) had the greatest number of individuals (Appendix 2, Transect 7). Other common species were *Prunus integrifolia* (Rosaceae), *Diatenopterix sorbifolia* (Sapindaceae), *Tabebuia lapacho* (Bignoniaceae), Lauraceae sp., *Ximenia americana* (Olacaceae), and *Roupala montana* (Proteaceae). Emergents were *Tabebuia lapacho* (Bignoniaceae) and *Myroxylon peruiferum* (Fabaceae). Though no individuals occurred in our transects, we observed several emergent specimens, measured to 115 cm dbh, of *Tipuana tipu* (Fabaceae) in the area. The understory was very well developed and thick, with *Pteris deflexa* (Pteridophyta), *Psychotria yungasensis* and *Palicourea* sp. (Rubiaceae), *Miconia calvescens* (Melastomataceae), *Justicia* sp. (Acanthaceae) and stands of *Stromanthe* sp. (Marantaceae). Epiphytes were very abundant and included *Vriesea maxoniana* and *Fosterella albicans* (Bromeliaceae), *Peperomia silvarum* (Piperaceae) and pendent mosses (*Pilotrichella pentasticha*).

Yet higher on the same ridge at approximately 1500 m, in an area where cattle seldom if ever reach, was another *Siphoneugena* forest, but with a high incidence of *Citrus* (Appendix 2, Transect 10). Other common species on the ridge were *Tabebuia lapacho* (Bignoniaceae), *Ilex argentina* (Aquifoliaceae), *Prunus* sp. (Rosaceae), *Myrcia* sp. (Myrtaceae), *Roupala meisneri* (Proteaceae), and *Aegiphila saltensis* (Verbenaceae). All of the *Ilex* seen on the ridge were large trees with dbh's > 30 cm. The high number of *Citrus* on the ridge may be because of higher level of disturbance, as in the forest only 20 m further down the slope only a single *Citrus* was found among 100 individual trees counted (Appendix 2, Transect 11).

This forest had the highest incidence of Citrus *invasion of any we had seen.*

Otherwise the forest on the slope had a similar species composition as on the ridge top with *Siphoneugena* accounting for the greatest number of individuals, followed by *Myrcia* sp. (Myrtaceae), *Cupania vernalis* (Sapindaceae), *Tabebuia lapacho* (Bignoniaceae), and *Aegiphila saltensis* (Verbenaceae). There were many lianas in this forest and shrubs in the area including *Psychotria* cf. *alba* and *Palicourea* sp. (Rubiaceae), *Rinorea* sp. (Violaceae), and dense stands of the bamboo *(Aulonemia* sp.), as well as *Celtis iguanaea* (Rulmaceae) and *Piper hieronymi* (Piperaceae); herbs included Poaceae, *Pteris deflexa* and *Polystichum* sp. (Pteridophyta) and *Stromanthe* sp. (Marantaceae), and *Polystichum* (Pteridophyta). Epiphytes on the ridge and nearby slopes included *Fosterella albicans* on tree trunks, *Tillandsia usneoides* (Bromeliaceae), and the abundant, pendent moss *Pilotrichella pentasticha*.

Higher up on the ridge, toward the base of the steep Cerro Tigrecillos wall, were stands of the tree fern *Alsophila incana* in moist, mossy *Siphoneugena* forest, much like that found at the base of Cerro Bufete to the south. In this same area were more open, grassy areas with abundant *Homolepis glutinosa* (Poaceae) and scattered shrubs and small trees of *Myrcianthes pseudomato* (Myrtaceae), *Styrax argenteus* (Styracaceae), *Ilex argentina* (Aquifoliaceae), *Urera altissima* (Urticaceae), *Allophyllus edulis* (Sapindaceae), and *Agarista boliviensis* (Ericaceae).

Cerro Tigrecillos

The mountain of Cerro Tigrecillos, called Serranía Alto Tayasurenda on the 1:250,000 map, is a horseshoe-shaped, mostly flat-topped mountain with vertical rock walls on the east, steep forested slopes on the south and west, and more gently sloping forested slopes to the north where the major drainage exits the plateau and flows into the Río Pejes, which shortly enters into the Río Pilcomayo. As far as we could tell, the summit of Cerro Tigrecillos was completely free of cattle grazing, and there were no *Citrus* trees found, very likely due to the high altitude. We measured the elevation on the summit at 2150 m, just a few hundred meters lower than Cerro Bufete.

The exposed, rocky ridges on the southwestern portion of the plateau had a dwarf (5-8 m tall), mossy forest with the lowest tree species diversity we found in any of our transects, with just 4 species counted among 100 trees > 30 cm dbh. These were *Ilex argentina* (Aquifoliaceae), *Clethra* aff. *scabra* (Clethraceae), *Symplocos* aff. *subcuneata* (Symplocaceae), and *Viburnum seemenii* (Caprifoliaceae). There were no emergent trees in this forest, perhaps as a result of high winds on the ridge. This composition closely matches the similar ridges at the same elevation near Cerro Bufete, and like that forest, the density of trees > 30 cm dbh was relatively high for the area with 100 individuals found in a transect of 65 x 10 m.

The understory was fairly open and included mostly herbaceous plants such as Cyperaceae, *Hydrocotyle humboldtii* (Apiaceae), *Chusquea* sp. (Poaceae), *Baccharis* sp. (Asteraceae), *Ichnanthus tenuis* (Poaceae), *Croton* aff. *saltensis* (Euphorbiaceae), and patches of *Lycopodium thyoides* and *L. clavatum* (Pteridophyta). Shrubs in the area included *Vallea stipularis* (Elaeocarpaceae), *Rhamnus sphaerosperma* (Rhamnaceae), *Miconia* sp., *Myrsine coriacea* (Myrsinaceae), *Randia* sp. and *Psychotria* sp. (Rubiaceae), and seedling trees of *Prunus* sp. (Rosaceae), *Podocarpus parlatorei* (Podocarpaceae), *Roupala meisneri* (Proteaceae), and Lauraceae.

Just off of the ridge, in a more protected area towards the center of the plateau to the east, a taller, denser, more diverse, semideciduous forest grows. The four species found along the nearby ridge were present in large numbers in this forest, but the trees tended to be larger in diameter, taller, and included some additional species: *Prunus tucumanensis* (Rosaceae), *Myrcia* cf. *multiflora* (Myrtaceae), *Crinondendron tucumanum* (Elaeocarpaceae), Lauraceae, *Podocarpus parlatorei* (Podocarpaceae), and *Rhamnus sphaerosperma* (Rhamnaceae). A common gray lichen gave the forest a characteristic appearance, especially noticeable on the deciduous trees.

El Palmar and Lower Río Urucuti Valley Vegetation

The lower Río Urucuti basin, between 900 and 1100 m, east of the Tucumano-Boliviano forest is transitional to the drier Serrano Chaqueño forests.

> *The exposed, rocky ridges on the plateau had a dwarf mossy forest.*

Most of the human population of the region lives in this area, which includes the settlements of El Palmar and Estancia La Redonda. This area has obvious signs of major habitat disturbances including logging, extensive cattle grazing, hog farming, and subsistence agriculture. A few protected pockets and areas along rocky river beds and low hills had tall semideciduous forest mostly composed of Mimosaceae and Myrtaceae (*Myrciaria* sp., *Eugenia uniflora*, cf. *Calycorectes psidiiflorus*, *Myrcianthes pungens*), a fairly open understory with many pteridophytes such as *Selaginella sulcata* (very common), *Asplenium formosum*, *Adiantopsis radiata*, *Adiantum raddianum*, *Asplenium* vel aff. *argentinum*, *Bolbitis serratifolia*, *Hemionitis tomentosa*, and *Peperomia blanda* (Piperaceae), *Callisia monandra* (Commelinaceae), *Justicia* sp. (Acanthaceae), *Cranichis* sp. (Orchidaceae), and *Petiveria alliacea* (Phytolaccaceae). The most common epiphyte was *Vriesea maxoniana* (Bromeliaceae), and the most common epiphytic orchids were *Isochilus linearis*, *Pleurothallis pubescens*, *P. obovata*, and *Stanhopea* sp.

The El Palmar valley has been altered extensively to provide pasture for cattle. *Citrus*, peanuts, cassava, and sugarcane are cultivated in unusual plots that are fenced in with a species of *Yucca*. Common trees in this area and adjacent low, rocky disturbed hills were *Tecoma stans* (Bignoniaceae), *Dilodendron bipinnatum* (Sapindaceae), *Acacia aroma*, *Anadenanthera macrocarpa* and *Pithecellobium scarale* (Mimosaceae), *Qualea* sp. (Vochysiaceae), *Myrsine coriacea* (Myrsinaceae), *Cordia alliodora* (Boraginaceae), and *Erythrina falcata* (Fabaceae). Common shrubs were *Psidium guineense* and *P. guajava* (Myrtaceae), *Dodonea viscosa* (Sapindaceae; often in pure stands), *Vernonanthura ferruginea* and *Cnicothamnus lorentzii* (Asteraceae), *Cordia curassavica* (Boraginaceae), *Maytenus ilicifolia* (Celastraceae), *Prisitimera andina* (Hippocrateaceae), and an unidentified species of Arecaceae. Common herbs were *Elephantopus mollis* and *Lepidaploa tarijensis* (Asteraceae), *Seemania gymnostoma* (Gesneriaceae), *Hyptis suaveolens*, *H. mutabilis*, and *Scutellaria purpurascens* (Lamiaceae), *Sida* aff. *glabra*

(Malvaceae), *Schizachyrium microstachyum* (Poaceae); and epiphytes were *Philodendron undulatum* (Araceae), *Aechmea distichantha*, *Tillandsia loliacea*, *T. tricholepis*, *T. didisticha*, *T. duratii*, and *T. tenuifolia* (Bromeliaceae).

AVIFAUNA OF CERRO BUFETE AND THE LOWER RÍO SANTA MARTHA BASIN, SOUTH CENTRAL CHUQUISACA (Thomas S. Schulenberg)

The department of Chuquisaca has remained, from the point of view of ornithology, one of the least-explored regions of Bolivia (Paynter 1992). In particular, the avifauna of montane forested portions of Chuquisaca essentially was unknown until very recently. Prior to the 1995 RAP expedition, the most important contribution to our knowledge of this forested zone was a series of surveys by Sjoerd Mayer and Jon Fjeldså across southern Chuquisaca in 1991 and 1992 (Fjeldså and Mayer 1996). These surveys complement those of the RAP expedition; combined, this recent field work has resulted in almost 90 new records of birds for Chuquisaca (see also Krabbe et al. 1996).

During the RAP survey birds were surveyed with binoculars and with tape-recorders and directional microphones. The presence of many bird species was documented with recordings, which will be deposited at the Library of Natural Sounds, Cornell Laboratory of Ornithology. We captured no birds with mist-nets for birds, although we made note of species that were captured in the mist-nets employed by the mammalogists. The survey took place at the beginning of the austral winter, so some migratory species were not present (Chesser 1994, Stotz et al. 1996) and levels of bird song were low. Although the survey was conducted late in the wet season, we experienced a number of days of inclement weather, especially when we were camped at Cerro Bufete.

At Cerro Bufete field work was concentrated in humid semideciduous forests above 1525 m, and on the habitats on the summit of Bufete and areas beyond. Somewhat drier forests below 1500 m, towards El Palmar, were sampled opportunistically only during the walks in and out of the

Chuquisaca has remained, from the point of view of ornithology, one of the least-explored regions of Bolivia.

field. In the Santa Martha basin we worked along the river itself, and along a narrow ridge ascending towards Cerro Tigrecillos.

Over 110 bird species were recorded during the survey (Appendix 3). Of these, over a quarter are species that were unknown from Chuquisaca prior to either our expedition, or the recent surveys by Mayer and Fjeldså (Remsen and Traylor 1989).

Bird species diversity in humid montane forests falls dramatically south of southern Santa Cruz. Among the montane species that are newly recorded for Chuquisaca, the majority of these fill in "holes" in the distribution of species previously known from localities both to the north (Santa Cruz) and to the south (Tarija or Argentina). On the other hand, several species newly recorded in Chuquisaca, such as *Scytalopus bolivianus* (Southern White-crowned Tapaculo), *Mionectes striaticollis* (Streak-necked Flycatcher), *Chlorophonia cyanea* (Blue-naped Chlorophonia), *Anisognathus flavinucha* (Blue-winged Mountain-Tanager), and *Piranga leucoptera* (White-winged Tanager), represent new southern records. Although montane forest species diversity is much lower in Chuquisaca than in areas farther north, nonetheless the presence of these species demonstrates that the forests near El Palmar are more humid and more diverse than are the better-known forests farther south.

An interesting northern range extension, and the most important ornithological discovery during the RAP survey, was of *Cinclus schulzi* (Rufous-throated Dipper) along the rivers that drain Cerro Bufete. This dipper first was reported along the Río Limonal by F. Guerra, and its presence was confirmed, at another site along the same river, by Schulenberg and Quirroga on 18 May. Later (24 May) an additional pair was seen along the Río Urucuti at the mouth of the Río Santa Martha, lower down along the same drainage system as the Limonal. The density of dippers in these mountains may be low; the species was not recorded at all in this region by earlier observers, even though it was specifically sought after (S. Mayer, pers. comm.), and we did not see it elsewhere along the Río Santa Martha. This species previously was known only from extreme northern Argentina and from Tarija. It is confined to clear, fast streams and rivers; the

extent of water pollution in northern Argentina has led to concern about this poorly-known, and apparently rare, bird (Collar et al. 1992, Tyler 1994).

Although montane species diversity is low, Chuquisaca is within a small center of endemism for montane species (Cracraft 1985, Stotz et al. 1996). Virtually all of these endemic species were recorded in the regions west and north of El Palmar. Three of these endemics are potentially threatened species. A previously unknown population of one of these species, *Cinclus schulzi*, was discovered during the RAP survey. Apparently significant populations of the two other threatened regional endemics, *Penelope dabbenei* and *Amazona tucumana*, were reported (Fjeldså and Mayer 1996) at higher elevations in mountains west of Cerro Bufete. Thus, the humid montane forests west and north of El Palmar in south central Chuquisaca represent one of the best conservation opportunities in Bolivia for this avifauna.

MAMMALS OF THE RÍO URUCUTI BASIN, SOUTH CENTRAL CHUQUISACA, BOLIVIA (L. H. Emmon)

Overview

The tendril of moist forest that extends along the eastern Andean slope for a length of about 670 km, between the end of the Yungas of Bolivia south to Jujuy, Argentina, seems to have a narrow elevational range (between 900 m and 2800 m at most), on steep terrain sandwiched between the dry upper "Valles" and lowland dry forests. This forest, the Bosque Tucumano-Boliviano, is located in the region where the Andes make an abrupt 110° turn at Amboró in Bolivia, and commence to run slightly east of straight south. The absolute area of this forest is small, as it is probably at most 40 km wide (but usually much narrower), and is fragmented by intervening dry valleys.

A preliminary list of the mammals known from this forest was compiled from the literature and from some museum records; because the taxonomy of several rodents has been revised subsequent to

The most important ornithological discovery during the RAP survey was of Cinclus schulzi.

some publications, there is ambiguity about the identity of several rodents and small marsupials listed in previous publications in Argentina. We emphasize that the species list for Bosque Tucumano-Boliviano (Appendix 4) is approximate, and best is used to show general trends. The geographic ranges of the rodents and marsupials are poorly known, from few collections. Without reviewing each specimen, it is impossible to determine whether names used by different collectors refer to the same forms. The akodontine rodents, in particular, are extremely speciose and difficult to identify, and new species are frequently discovered. Some of the *Akodon* that we collected have proven difficult to characterize (P. Myers, pers comm). Furthermore, the southernmost extension of this biogeographical area, in Jujuy and a small part of Salta Province, Argentina, has received the most biological study, including a mammal list based on 20 years of records (Olrog 1979); studies of the single primate within the region (Brown 1983); and annotated records of the included species (Ojeda and Mares 1989). A number of expeditions have made collections in the region in Bolivia. Most of the results of these expeditions remain unpublished, however, but some records are listed in Anderson (1993) and in various taxonomic works on individual taxa (Cook et al. 1990; Anderson 1989; Myers and Carleton 1981; Myers and Patton 1989a; Myers and Patton 1989b; Myers et al. 1990).

This preliminary list (Appendix 4) nonetheless has several striking features. The Bosque Tucumano-Boliviano is not rich in mammal species, with a total of only about 66 species reported from the area (but the results of some expeditions have not been published). Lists from well-studied regions in Argentina include only 42 species (Olrog 1979) and 43 species (Ojeda and Mares 1989). We recorded 30 species (Appendix 5) on our expedition to the vicinity of El Palmar, but the list includes a few lowland species that may not properly belong to the fauna of the moist forest band. It is certain that insectivorous bats are significantly under represented in all existing lists, but nonetheless, the overall mammal diversity is low. The lists show that the fauna is quite homogenous throughout the area, from at least Chuquisaca south to Salta and Jujuy, and this region defines a distinct mammalian biogeographic unit. We did not determine whether the higher elevation habitats (puna) also have uniform species composition within the same latitude range. The fauna of this part of Bolivia is very poorly known, as evidenced by the fact that at least 10 of the species we encountered are not represented by specimens from the Department of Chuquisaca (Anderson 1993), and at least half of the species of bats and marsupials collected are new for the department.

The mammal fauna of the Bosque Tucumano-Boliviano is poor in large mammals and bats (Appendix 4), with 1 species of primate, 3 of large ungulates, 1 large rodent species, and 17 species of bats. The region is rich in carnivores (14 species), however, and in small rodents (23 species). Ten of the small rodents (43%) appear to be endemic to the region. One of the marsupials, *Micoureus constantiae budini*, also is an endemic taxon, which in our opinion may deserve species status, while the local population of another marsupial, *Lutreolina*, also is distinctive and probably merits description as a new species (Olrog 1979, pers. obs.). Of the 66 mammal species in the fauna of the Bosque Tucumano-Boliviano, then, at least 11 species (17%) are endemic, all of which are rodents and marsupials. With the exceptions of the spectacled bear and pampas cat, all of the larger mammals and bats, in contrast, are widespread lowland Amazonian species. Consequently, the level of endemism is extremely high among the truly montane species of the fauna.

This high level of endemism gives this small mammal fauna an importance far out of proportion to its known size. We suspect that an even greater level of endemism will be discovered when the fauna is better inventoried and the systematics of rodents and marsupials better understood.

Methods

Small mammals were trapped using three sizes of H. B. Sherman live traps (small, large and extra large, 53 total). Trapping was carried out at two sites: Cerro Bufete (12-19 May 1995; 351 trap/nights) and Limón (24-28 May 1995; 265 trap/nights), for a total of 616 trap/nights.

The level of endemism is extremely high among the truly montane species of the fauna.

Trapping success was high at El Bufete (around 2000 m), with 59 captures of rodents and marsupials (17%), chiefly montane species; while it was very low at Limón (trapline at 900 m), with only 4 captures (1%) of lowland species. Collections from trapping included 46 rats (eight species) and four marsupials (two species). Bats were captured by mist netting on eight nights, but poor weather conditions (continual rain, cold, and moonlight) greatly hampered our efforts, and only 17 bats were caught. Squirrels were collected with a shotgun by Fernando Guerra, who also helped us to net bats. Large mammals were identified by direct observation and from tracks. The beaches of the Río Santa Martha were a particularly fruitful source of tracks. Day and night observation walks to look for mammals were undertaken at largely at Limón (25 h), with a small effort at El Bufete (3.5 h).

Details of the mammal fauna

We recorded 30 species during our short expedition to the vicinity of El Palmar (Appendix 5), although the list includes a few lowland species that may not properly belong in the fauna of the moist forest band.

A surprising finding to us was the absence of montane bat species, apart from *Sturnira erythromos,* a small frugivore. Perhaps the vegetation of Bosque Tucumano-Boliviano does not provide year-round fruit and nectar for the montane glossophagines and stenodermatines that are common on the more northerly Andean slopes, or perhaps sampling thus far has not been adequate to discover them. There seems to be an abrupt decline in phyllostomid bat species richness below the great bend in the Andes.

Unlike bats, rodents seem to undergo no loss of species (although some genera seem to be absent), but rather experience a turnover and replacement by a new set. Marsupials seem to show a dropout of the mouse opossum genus *Marmosops,* and perhaps *Gracilinanus,* leaving four genera closely allied to lowland dry forest and open habitat forms, suggesting that these taxa invaded the Andean slopes from below rather than originating in the northern Andes. Because small

marsupials have erratic population densities, some species may have eluded inventory in this region.

Andean bears have been recorded along the Andean slope of Bolivia to nearly the Argentine border (Salazar and Anderson 1990), but there are no verified Argentine records, and these southernmost populations are not protected within any parks or reserves south of Parque Nacional Amboró. There may be a close habitat association between Andean bears and bromeliads, of which they feed on the hearts (Peyton 1980). Brown capuchin monkeys (*Cebus apella*), the only primate on the Andean slope within Bosque Tucumano-Boliviano, feeds intensively on bromeliad hearts in Argentina (Brown 1983, Chalukian et al. 1982), and we likewise saw them doing so at Limón on this expedition. The physical strength of these two species allows them to use this well protected resource, which must be ripped apart, and thus they can survive in habitats that perhaps are otherwise marginal or inhospitable to frugivores. Protection of bromeliads, which may be totally destroyed by fire, may be important for conservation of these two mammals in this zone. The lack of phyllostomid bats also suggests at least a seasonal scarcity of fruits. However, livestock grazing in the forest understory may have reduced or destroyed local populations of understory fruiting shrubs and treelets.

We saw evidence (nutshells opened by squirrels) that the endemic Argentine squirrel (*Sciurus argentineus;* see taxonomic notes in Appendix 4) feeds on the nuts of "nogales" (walnuts, *Juglans* spp.) that are a feature of this forest type throughout its length. This squirrel has much stouter incisors for its size than any other Bolivian species. It also feeds on ears of maize (we collected the squirrels in a cornfield), but probably only where forest closely borders the fields.

Although we were able to sample only a small range of habitats, there was some habitat separation between different *Akodon* species: most specimens of *A. fumeus* and of *A.* (*Hypsimys*) sp. were captured within pastured forest that had much grassy and herbaceous understory with *Chusquea* bamboo. *Akodon siberiae*, the rarest species, was captured in open, rocky, grassland/shrubland on the face of Cerro Bufete, along with

Oligoryzomys nigripes and *Oxymycterus inca*. Nonetheless, there was some habitat overlap between all *Akodon* forms.

Most of the mammalian endemics seem to occupy the higher elevation, wettest forest and rock slopes, but we were not able to sample all habitats.

Conservation implications

Our overflights showed that only two large areas of forest remain on the Bolivian Andean slope of the region we are considering, along with many fragmented forests interspersed with croplands and pasture. Fire evidently has deforested many uncultivated steep slopes by escaping from agricultural burns and sweeping uphill. Some of the endemic mammal species of the region require forest (*Micoureus,* squirrels and other arboreal rodents), but for most of the small terrestrial rodents too little is known of their habitat needs to well predict the outcome of forest degradation or elimination. We can be certain nonetheless that some species surely will be extirpated, as forests decline in extent, while other species might survive or even increase. Clearly monkeys, bears, tapirs, otters, and jaguar depend on the continued persistence for forest. Another obvious threat is that of wholesale replacement of native trees by feral oranges. Ironically, *Cebus* monkeys may be agents in the dispersal of oranges, as they feed on the fruits and are likely to disperse seeds, unlike the squirrels and parrots, which feed on the seeds.

The chief disturbance to the forest we visited is the pasturing of cattle in the forest understory. This may be a major factor contributing to the spread of feral oranges, as cattle may feed on and destroy the seedings of native trees, leaving orange seedlings without competition. The local people do not seem to do much subsistence hunting, and the principal threat to the fauna is from habitat destruction.

Argentina values its Bosque Tucumano-Boliviano highly, preserving it in three national parks: P. N. Baritú (44,000 ha), P. N. Calilegua (76,000 ha), and P. N. El Rey (72,000 ha). Many of the moist forest species such as monkeys, porcupines, climbing rats, and woolly mouse opossums, have their southernmost extensions at El Rey or Calilegua, near the Jujuy-Salta border. They do not reach into the Province of Tucumán, from which the forest gets its name.

The Bosque Tucumano-Boliviano within Bolivia deserves some form of protection, so that an entire habitat type and group of species does not disappear from that country. Preservation could be in a form other than a park, but one that would not allow commercial logging, and would limit grazing to no more than its current extent. The best prospect for a protected zone would be the steep, inaccessible hanging basin of the upper Urucuti watershed, which is naturally protected. Moreover, it is an important water catchment for the Río Pilcomayo, which will suffer water reduction if more of its headwaters are deforested.

REPTILES AND AMPHIBIANS FROM THE VICINITY OF EL PALMAR IN THE ANDES OF CHUQUISACA (M. B. Harvey)

The composition of amphibian assemblages in wet central Andean forests has been fairly well documented for sites in Argentina (see especially Cei 1980 and citations therein, Carrizo 1992) and, recently, along the eastern Andean slopes or "yungas" of Bolivia north of about 18°S (De la Riva 1991, 1992, 1993, 1994, Harvey and Smith 1993, 1994, Harvey and Keck 1995, Harvey 1996, Reynolds and Foster 1992). Fewer reports on the reptiles of the yungas have appeared in recent years (Reynolds and Foster 1992), while the distributions of reptiles in wet forests of Argentina have been summarized by Cei (1993). For the herpetofauna of the Bolivian Andes, several recent lists (De la Riva 1990, Fugler 1986, 1989) summarize distributional data appearing in older publications.

Almost completely absent from the literature are any references to the herpetofauna of the eastern Andean slopes in Chuquisaca and Tarija, Bolivia. Such information is desperately needed as humanity encroaches on the remaining islands of the Bosque Tucumano-Boliviano in these departments. If the herpetofauna in these forests approaches the diversity and endemism observed

We can be certain that some species surely will be extirpated, as forests decline in extent.

in forests further north, many species will become extinct with as their habitat is destroyed. However, if the fauna of these forests lacks endemic species, conservation funding might be better spent protecting more valuable areas elsewhere.

Methods and Results

This study is based on 32 species (Appendix 5) collected by the author, J. Fernando Guerra S., and other members of the RAP team in the vicinity of El Palmar, Provincia Sud Cinti, Departamento de Chuquisaca, Bolivia during a 28 day period ending 1 June 1995. Each of the 32 species was collected in one or more of the following habitats:

1) Montane Meadows—Heavily grazed and deforested areas atop Cerro Bufete and adjacent ridges, 2300-2500 meters, including pasture, elfin forests, rock outcrops, and streams.

2) Subtropical Wet Forest—Forest covering the slopes of Cerro Bufete and along the Río Santa Martha, 1150-2050 meters, including a variety of forest types, all slightly to heavily grazed by livestock.

3) Mountain Streams—Streams cascading down slopes of Cerro Bufete and adjacent mountains.

4) Forest Edge—Species assigned to this category were collected only along the edge of the forest in the El Palmar valley.

5) El Palmar Valley—Disturbed area around El Palmar, 900-1150 meters, including pasture, rock outcrops, temporary ponds, and streams.

Each of these five habitats was thoroughly searched by raking through leaf litter, turning rocks and fallen logs, and carefully scanning the ground and vegetation during the day and night (sundown to midnight).

Two-hundred-sixty-six voucher specimens, representing all species except *Liophis ceii*, were fixed in 10% formalin and preserved in 70% alcohol. These specimens are deposited in the University of Texas at Arlington Collection of Vertebrates, Arlington, Texas and the Colección Boliviana de Fauna, La Paz, Bolivia. Sampling was biased toward the collection of as many species as possible. For this reason, data are

insufficient for developing a diversity index for any habitat or making similar quantitative comparisons. Such indices require a measure of relative abundance in addition to numbers of species within each habitat and require greater control on collecting bias than was exercised.

The species composition at El Palmar was compared qualitatively to that of wet forests near Entre Rios, Tarija (63°13'W; 21°29'S; 1900 meters) and La Yunga, Santa Cruz (63°54'W; 18°06'S; 1900-2200 meters) based on data taken by the author in 1994 (Tarija) and 1991-94 (La Yunga). Comparisons based on presence or absence of species at different sites are complicated by numerous factors affecting some species' activity patterns such as time of year, temperature, and amount of rainfall. Reptiles were collected too rarely to use when comparing species compositions among the sites. Both Entre Rios and La Yunga were visited during the wet summer months of December and January, whereas El Palmar was visited during the fall months of May and June. However, overall physiognomy and weather patterns were very similar, at least during the time collections were made at the three sites. Moreover, locals informed the author that prior to the RAP team's arrival, no "winter weather" had reached the El Palmar valley. At both La Yunga and El Palmar rain fell frequently and temperatures dropped during nightly collecting hours to around 10-12°C. A light rain (less than 5 cm accumulation) fell only once during the four days spent at Entre Rios. Each of the three sites is covered in wet montane forest traversed by scattered streams and has been partially degraded by cattle and other livestock. At each of the three sites, the author worked with a second experienced herpetologist to assemble the collections for which comparisons are based.

The herpetofauna in the forests and disturbed areas surrounding El Palmar is a transitional fauna between the yungas and the wet forests in northern Argentina. El Palmar's relatively depauperate herpetofauna exhibits four biogeographic patterns:

1) Species occurring in the yungas of Bolivia and Peru but not reaching northern Argentina; all are restricted to mountain streams.

Bufo veraguensis, Cochranella bejaranoi,

Telmatobius simonsi, Hyla armata.

2) Central Andean Species. Species having distributions in northern Argentina and extending to southern Peru; all are adaptable species and enter drier, nonforest environments in at least some parts of their range. Carrillo de Espinoza and Icochea (1995) greatly extended the range of *Opipeuter xestus* when they reported it from Junín, Peru. They did not indicate whether they examined any specimens on which to base this surprising range extension. *Opipeuter xestus* otherwise is known from Argentina, and from Cochabamba, La Paz, and Santa Cruz in Bolivia.

Gastrotheca marsupiata, Hyla callipleura, Hyla pulchella, Opipeuter xestus, Pantodactylus schiebersi parkeri, Tropidurus melanopleurus.

3) Species ranging from Argentina to Santa Cruz and southern Cochabamba, Bolivia but apparently absent from wet forests of the yungas. Species in this category reach their northern distributional limit in the dry intermontane valleys of Santa Cruz and southern Cochabamba such as the valley surrounding the western border of Parque Nacional Amboró between Samaipata and Comarapa, Santa Cruz. *Eleutherodactylus discoidalis* was reported from La Yunga and Cuevas by De la Riva (1993), although he did not state whether the species occurs in wet forest or in the dry formations on the western slopes at these sites. The species is otherwise unknown from the wet forests of the yungas.

Scinax castroviejoi, Eleutherodactylus discoidalis, Liophis ceii, Philodryas varias, Stenocercus marmoratus (this last species, though not reported from Argentina, occurs at Entre Rios, Tarija not far from the Argentinean border).

4) Chacoan species that invade the Andean foothills. Species in this category include those distributed within the Gran Chaco or that occur in dry forests surrounding the Gran Chaco.

Bufo sp. 2 (*typhonius* group), *Hyla minuta, Leptodactylus chaquensis, Leptodactylus gracilis, Odontophrynus americanus, Elachistocleis ovalis, Chironius exoletus, Liophis typhlus, Liophis sagittifer, Philodryas psammophideus, Waglerophis merremii, Stenocercus caducus, Bothrops neuwiedi.*

Too little information is known about the new

species encountered during this expedition to assign them to one of these categories, although they most likely are part of the third assemblage. They currently are known only from the vicinity of El Palmar and may be endemic to this area. However, this is unlikely because both new species were found in dry, unforested areas.

The amphibian fauna of El Palmar is much less diverse than that inhabiting the southern yungas. This drop in species is best illustrated by a comparison of leaf-litter inhabiting frogs. Like many localities further north in Bolivia and Peru, eleutherodactyline frogs form the most speciose component of the southern yungas anuran fauna. Six species of eleutherodactyline leptodactylids are common at La Yunga (*Eleutherodactylus fenestratus, E. fraudator, E. platydactylus, E. rhabdolaemus, E.* sp., and *Ischnocnema sanctaecrucis*) and five others are rare at La Yunga or known from adjacent localities such as the Serranía de Siberia in southern Cochabamba (*Eleutherodactylus cruralis, E. discoidalis, E. mercedesae, Phrynopus kempffi,* and *Phyllonastes* sp.). In contrast, this assemblage reduces to one common species, *Eleutherodactylus discoidalis,* at El Palmar, Entre Rios, and northern Argentina. Similarly, at La Yunga, two leaf litter inhabiting members of the *Bufo veraguensis* group occur (*B. justinianoi* and *B. quechua*). Both appear to be absent from El Palmar, *B. veraguensis* being the only member of the group encountered at this locality. Interestingly, *Bufo veraguensis* was commonly found away from streams at La Yunga, but never away from streams at El Palmar.

The stream-inhabiting anurans of the yungas extend south to El Palmar but were not found at Entre Rios. At both La Yunga and El Palmar, *Bufo veraguensis, Hyla armata, Hyla callipleura, Telmatobius simonsi,* and *Cochranella bejaranoi* make up a group of common stream inhabiting amphibians. Rarer species like *Bufo amboroensis* and *Telmatobius yuracare* were not found at either El Palmar or La Yunga, but occur in low densities at a few cloud forests in Santa Cruz and Cochabamba (Harvey and Smith 1993, De la Riva 1994).

As detailed above, the herpetofauna occurring in the forests and disturbed areas around El

The herpeto-fauna in areas surrounding El Palmar is a transitional fauna between the yungas and the wet forests in northern Argentina.

Palmar is a combination of (1) yungas species, (2) adaptable species with wide ranges extending from Argentina to Cochabamba or Peru, (3) species distributed in dry environments and associated forests in the Andean foothills from Argentina to Santa Cruz and Cochabamba, and (4) species that invade the Andean foothills from the lowlands. With the perhaps unlikely exception of the two undescribed reptiles, all of these species are protected in reserves elsewhere in Bolivia and Argentina, especially within Parque Nacional Amboró and The Gran Chaco reserve. Currently the species of my biogeographic categories 1 and 2 occur within Parque Nacional Noel Kempff, and those of category 4 are probably common in the Gran Chaco reserve.

Some species such as *Leptodactylus gracilis* and *Liophis ceii* occur within nature reserves in Argentina but may not be adequately protected within Bolivia. These species occur in the vicinity of the El Fuerte ruins and probably in the limited dry montane area within Parque Nacional Amboró, but suitable habitats for these species are small in both parks and may not be large enough to support reproductively viable populations. Expanding the borders of Parque Nacional Amboró to include more of the valley containing Samaipata and Comarapa would protect the habitat of the remaining species listed in category 3 as well as species with limited distributions in the dry Andean valleys of Santa Cruz and Cochabamba such as *Bothrops jonathani* (Harvey 1994) and *Philodryas* sp. (=*Philodryas aestivus* subsp. in Thomas [1976] and currently being described as a full species; Thomas, personal communication).

The expedition to El Palmar failed to find an assemblage of reptiles and amphibians comparable in diversity and local endemism to that of the yungas. Such an area may exist on the eastern slopes of the Andes between Samaipata and El Palmar, and I urge that additional herpetological surveys be conducted in this section of the Andes.

LITERATURE CITED

Agreda C., E., et al. 1994. Estudio de Chuquisaca. Suelos y Riegos. Corporación Regional de Desarrollo de Chuquisaca, Departamento de Recursos Naturales. Sucre: Bolivia.

Anderson, S. 1993. Los mamiferos bolivianos: notas de distribución y claves de identificación. La Paz: Instituto de Ecología.

Anderson, S., and N. Olds. 1989. Notes on Bolivian mammals. 5. Taxonomy and distribution of *Bolomys* (Muridae, Rodentia). American Museum Novitates No. 2935.

Brown, A. D. 1983. Distribución y conservación de *Cebus apella* (Cebidae: Primates) en el Noroeste Argentino. La Primatologia en Latinoamerica: Anales del Simposio de Primatologia del IX Congresso Latinoamericano de Zoología, Arequipa, Peru.

Brown, A. D., S. C. Chalukian, and L. M. Malmierca. 1985. Estudio floristico-estructural de un sector de selva semidecidua del noroeste argentino. I. Composicion floristica, densidad y diversidad. Darwiniana 26:27-41.

Brown, A. D., S. Chalukian, L. Malmierca, and O. Colillas. 1982. Habitat structure and feeding behavior of *Cebus apella* in "El Rey" National Park, Argentina. International Journal of Primatology 3:265.

Cabrera, A. L. 1956. Esquema fitogeográfico de la Republica Argentina. Revista del Museo de la Plata, Sección Botánica 8:112-113.

Cabrera, A. L. 1976. Regiones fitogeográficas Argentinas. Enciclopedia Argentina de Agricultura y Jardineria. Ed. 2(1):1-85.

Carrillo de Espinoza, N., and J. Icochea. 1995. Lista taxonomica preliminar de los reptiles vivientes del Peru. Publicaciones del Museo de Historia Natural, Universidad Nacional Mayor de San Marcos (A) 49:1-27.

Carrizo, G. R. 1992. Cuatro especies nuevas de anuros (Bufonidae: *Bufo* e Hylidae: *Hyla*) del norte de la Argentina. Cuadernos de Herpetologia 7:14-23.

Cei, J. M. 1980. Amphibians of Argentina. Monografia 2. Torino, Italy: Museo Regionale di Scienze Naturali - Torino.

Cei, J. M. 1993. Reptiles del noroeste, nordeste y este de la Argentina: herpetofauna de las selvas subtropicales, puna y pampas. Monogafia 14. Torino, Italy: Museo Regionale di Scienze Naturali - Torino.

Chalukian, S. 1991. Regeneración, sucesión y plantas invasoras en Las Yungas, Salta, Argentina. Masters Thesis, Programa Regional de Manejo de Vida Silvestra, Heredia, Costa Rica. Abstract in Yungas 2(1):4-6. 1992.

Collar, N. J., L. P. Gonzaga, N. Krabbe, A. Madroño Nieto, L. G. Naranjo, T. A. Parker III, and D. C. Wege. 1992. Threatened birds of the Americas: the ICBP/IUCN Red Data Book. Cambridge, U. K.: International Council for Bird Preservation.

Cook, J. A., S. Anderson, and T. L. Yates. 1990. Notes on Bolivian mammals 6. The genus *Ctenomys* (Rodentia, Ctenomyidae) in the highlands. American Museum Novitates No. 2980.

Chesser, R. T. 1994. Migration in South America: an overview of the austral system. Bird Conservation International 4:91-107.

Cracraft, J. 1985. Historical biogeography and patterns of differentiation within the South American avifauna: areas of endemism. Pp. 49-84 In: Buckley, P. A., M. S. Foster, E. S. Morton, R. S. Ridgely, and F. G. Buckley (Eds.). Neotropical Ornithology. Ornithological Monographs No. 36. Washington, D.C.: American Ornithologists' Union.

De la Riva, I. 1990. Lista preliminar comentada de los anfibios de Bolivia con datos sobre su distribución. Bollettino del Museo Regionale di Scienze Naturali Torino 8:261- 319.

De la Riva, I. 1991. Comentarios sobre el género *Gastrotheca* (Anura: Hylidae) en Bolivia y descripción de una nueva especie. Revista Española de Heretología 6:15-22.

De la Riva, I. 1993. Sinopsis del género *Eleutherodactylus* (Amphibia, Anura, Leptodactylidae) en Bolivia y adición de tres especies nuevas para el país. Revista Española de Herpetología 7:97-105.

De la Riva, I. 1994. A new aquatic frog of the genus *Telmatobius* (Anura: Leptodactylidae) from Bolivian cloud forests. Herpetologica 50:38-45.

Duellman, W. E., and R. Schulte, 1992. Description of a new species of *Bufo* from northern Peru with comments on phenetic groups of South American toads (Anura: Bufonidae). Copeia 1992:162-172.

Fjeldså, J., and S. Mayer. 1996. Recent ornithological surveys in the Valles region, southern Bolivia and the possible role of Valles for the evolution of the Andean avifauna. Technical Report 1. Rønde, Denmark: Centre for Research on the Cultural and Biological Diversity of Andean Rainforests (DIVA).

Foster, R. B. 1993. A variable transect method for rapid assessment of tropical plant communities. Unpublished manuscript. Chicago: Environmental and Conservation Programs, Field Museum of Natural History; and

Washington, D.C.: Conservation Biology, Conservation International.

Fugler, C. M. 1986. Una lista preliminar de las serpientes de Bolivia. Ecología en Bolivia 8:45-72.

Fugler, C. M. 1989. Lista preliminar de saurios. Ecología en Bolivia 13:57-75.

Grau, A. 1985. La expansion del Aliso del Cerro (*Alnus acuminata* H.B.K. subsp. *acuminata)* en el noroeste de Argentina. Lilloa 36: 237-247.

Grau, H. R. and A. D. Brown. 1995. Patterns of tree species diversity along latitudinal and altitudinal gradients in the Argentinean subtropical montane forests. Pp. 295-300 In: Churchill, S. P., H. Balslev, E. Forero, and J. L. Lutyen (Eds.), Biodiversity and Conservation of Neotropical Montane Forests. New York: New York Botanical Garden.

Harvey, M. B. 1994. A new species of montane pitviper (Serpentes: Viperidae: *Bothrops*) from Cochabamba, Bolivia. Proceedings of the Biological Society of Washington 107:60-66.

Harvey, M. B. 1996. A new species of glass frog (Anura: Centrolenidae: *Cochranella)* from Bolivia and the taxonomic status of *Cochranella flavidigitata*. Herpetologica 52:427-435.

Harvey, M. B., and M. B. Keck. 1995. A new species of *Ischnocnema* (Anura: Leptodactylidae) from high elevations in the Andes of Central Bolivia. Herpetologica 51:56-66.

Harvey, M. B., and E. N. Smith. 1993. A new species of aquatic *Bufo* (Anura: Bufonidae) from cloud forests in the Serranía de Siberia, Bolivia. Proceedings of the Biological Society of Washington 106:442-449.

Harvey, M. B., and E. N. Smith. 1994. A new species of *Bufo* (Anura: Bufonidae) from cloud forests in Bolivia. Herpetologica 50:32-38.

Killeen, T. J., E. Garcia E., and S. G. Beck (Eds.). 1993. Guia de Arboles de Bolivia. La Paz, Bolivia: Herbario Nacional de Bolivia; and St. Louis: Missouri Botanical Garden.

Krabbe, N., B. O. Poulsen, A. Frølander, M. Hinojosa B., and C. Quiroga O. 1996. Birds of montane forest fragments in Chuquisaca Department, Bolivia. Bulletin of the British Ornithologists' Club 116:230-243.

Meyer, T. 1963. Estudios sobre la selva Tucumana. Opera Lilloana 10:1-144.

Moyano, M. Y., and C. P. Movia. 1989. Relevamiento fisonomico-estructural de la vegetacion de las Sierras de San Javier and El Periquillo. Lilloa 37:123-135.

Musser, G. G., and M. D. Carleton. 1992. Family Muridae. In: D. E. Wilson and D. M. Reeder (Eds.). Mammal species of the World: A geographic and taxonomic reference. Washington, D.C.: Smithsonian Institution Press.

Myers, P. 1989. A preliminary revision of the *varius* group of *Akodon* (*A. dayi, dolores, molinae, neocenus, simulator, toba,* and *varius*). Pp. 5-543 In: K. H. Redford and J. F. Eisenberg (Eds.), Advances in Neotropical Mammalogy. Gainesville: Sandhill Crane Press.

Myers, P., and M. D. Carleton. 1981. The species of *Oryzomys* (*Oligoryzomys*) in Paraguay and the identity of Azara's "rat sixième ou rat à tarse noire". Miscellaneous Publications, Museum of Zoology, University of Michigan No. 161.

Myers, P., and J. L. Patton. 1989a. A new species of *Akodon* from the cloud forests of eastern Cochabamba Department, Bolivia (Rodentia: Sigmodontinae). Occasional Papers of the Museum of Zoology, University of Michigan No. 720.

Myers, P., and J. L. Patton. 1989b. *Akodon* of Peru and Bolivia—Revision of the *fumeus* group (Rodentia: Sigmodontinae). Occasional Papers of the Museum of Zoology, University of Michigan No. 721.

Myers, P., J. L. Patton, and M. F. Smith. 1990. A review of the *boliviensis* group of *Akodon* (Muridae: Sigmodontinae), with emphasis on Peru and Bolivia. Miscellaneous Publications, Museum of Zoology, University of Michigan No. 177.

Ojeda, R. A., and M. A. Mares. 1989. A biogeographic analysis of the mammals of Salta Province, Argentina: Patterns of species assemblage in the Neotropics. Special Publications, The Museum of Texas Tech University No. 27.

Olrog, C. C. 1979. Los mamíferos de la selva humeda, Cerro Calilegua, Jujuy. Acta Zoologica Lilloana 33: 9-14.

Paynter, R. A., Jr. 1992. Ornithological gazetteer of Bolivia. Cambridge, Massachusetts: Museum of Comparative Zoology.

Peyton, B. 1980. Ecology, distribution, and food habits of spectacled bears, *Tremarctos ornatus*, in Peru. Journal of Mammalogy 61:639-652.

Remsen, J. V., Jr., and M. A. Traylor, Jr. 1989. An annotated checklist of the birds of Bolivia. Vermillion, South Dakota:Buteo Books.

Reynolds, R. P., and M. S. Foster. 1992. Four new species of frogs and one new species of snake from the Chapare region of Bolivia with notes on other species. Herpetological Monographs 6:83-104.

Salazar, J., and S. Anderson. 1990. Informe sobre el estado actual del conocimiento del oso andino en Bolivia. Ecología en Bolivia 15: 3-23.

Stotz, D. F., J. W. Fitzpatrick, T. A. Parker III, and D. K. Moskovits, Neotropical birds:ecology and conservation. Chicago:University of Chicago Press.

Thomas, O. 1921. On a further collection of mammals from Jujuy obtained by Sr. E. Budin. Annals and Magazine of Natural History, Series 9, 8:608-617.

Thomas, R. A. 1976. A revision of the South American colubrid snake genus *Philodryas* Wagler, 1830. Unpublished Ph.D. thesis. College Station, Texas: Texas Agricultural and Mechanical University.

Tyler, S. J. 1994. The Yungas of Argentina: in search of Rufous-throated Dippers *Cinclus schulzi*. Cotinga No. 2:38-41.

Wilson, D. E., and D. M., Eds. 1992. Mammal species of the World: A taxonomic and geographic reference. Washington, D.C.: Smithsonian Institution Press.

GAZETTEER AND ITINERARY

BOLIVIA: DEPARTAMENTO DE CHUQUISACA, PROVINCIA DE SUD CINTI.

Coordinates were taken with Trimble® hand-held GPS receivers, map datum WPS-84.

El Palmar. 20°51.05' S, 64°19.16' W, 1170 m. A small town with a rough airstrip (but no road for motorized vehicles). In a treeless, wide flat valley.

Cerro Bufete. 20°49.81' S, 64°22.47' W, 2000 m. Camp in pastured forest on the ridgetop at the base of the "wall" of the table mountain Cerro Bufete (local name 'El Bujete'), along the main trail from El Palmar to Culpina. From here we worked up and down the same ridge; in the forested valley below to the north; and above on the deforested grassy tableland and its forest patches.

Río Santa Martha. 20°43.73' S, 64°17.89' W, 900 m. 13.68 km, 09° true N from El Palmar. Camp on riverside, night of 23 May.

Limón (Camp Garrapata). 20°42.69' S, 64°18.32' W, 950 m. 15.57 km, 7° true N from El Palmar. Camp on Río Santa Martha, from which we worked upriver along the river bed; and up the ridge bordering the Río Santa Martha on the north, past the highest cleared *chaco* (field) and pastured forest at 1,320 m elevation, to the summit of Cerro Tigrecillo. The uppermost portion of this trail was cut during the expedition.

Cerro Tigrecillo. 20°39.35' S, 64°20.37' W, 2150 m. Camp in elfin forest on the summit of table mountain.

ITINERARY

5 May: Harvey, Hesse, Guerra and support personnel arrive in El Palmar.

8 May: Harvey, Hesse, Guerra and support personnel to Cerro Bufete.

11 May: Arroyo, Awbrey, Emmons, Holst, Jammes, Quirroga, Schulenberg and Serrano arrive in El Palmar.

12 May: Arroyo, Awbrey, Emmons, Holst, Jammes, Quirroga, Schulenberg and Serrano to Cerro Bufete.

14 May: Awbrey and Jammes to El Palmar.

16 May: Awbrey and Jammes to Santa Cruz.

21 May: Arroyo, Emmons, Guerra, Harvey, Hesse, Holst, Quirroga, Schulenberg and Serrano descend to El Palmar.

22 May: Arroyo, Emmons, Guerra, Harvey, Holst, Quirroga, Schulenberg and Serrano in El Palmar. Jammes arrives, and Hesse departs expedition.

23 May: Arroyo, Emmons, Guerra, Harvey, Holst, Jammes, Quirroga, Schulenberg and Serrano to Río Santa Martha.

24 May: Arroyo, Emmons, Guerra, Harvey, Holst, Jammes, Quirroga, Schulenberg and Serrano to Limón.

28 May: Arroyo, Guerra, Holst, Jammes, Quirroga and Serrano to Tigrecillo.

29 May: Harvey and Schulenberg to El Palmar; Guerra, Jammes and Quirroga to Limón.

30 May: Harvey and Schulenberg to Santa Cruz; Arroyo, Holst and Serrano to Limón; Guerra towards El Palmar on trail.

31 May: Arroyo, Emmons, Holst, Jammes, Quirroga and Serrano to El Palmar.

1 June: To Santa Cruz via Monteagudo.

APPENDICES

Plant Collections from the Río Urucuti Basin, South Central Chuquisaca, Bolivia

Martha Serrano, Luzmilla Arroyo Padilla, and Bruce K. Holst

Habitat type: TB = Bosque Tucumano-Boliviano (900-2500 m elevation); OA = Open areas on rock walls, grasslands, and steep, rocky, slopes on Cerro Bufete (2000-2600 m elevation); SC = Serrano-Chaqueño forest (850-1200 m elevation). Collector: BKH = Bruce K. Holst; LAP = Luzmilla Arroyo Padilla; MS = Martha Serrano.

TAXON	FOREST TYPE	COLLECTOR AND NUMBER
ACANTHACEAE		
Aphelandra hieronymi Griseb.	TB	LAP 916
Dicliptera aff. *tweediana* Nees	OA, TB	LAP 898; MS 1388
Justicia sp. 1	SC	BKH 4793
Justicia sp. 2	TB	BKH 4834
Ruellia cf. *graecizans* (Benth.) Schinz	TB	BKH 4842
Ruellia sanguinea Griseb.	TB	LAP 973
AMARANTHACEAE		
Alternanthera flavescens H.B.K.	SC	BKH 4922
Alternanthera aff. *lanceolata* (Benth.) Schinz	TB	LAP 919; MS 1290
Chamissoa maximiliani Mart. ex Moq.	SC	BKH 4893
Iresine diffusa Humb. & Bonpl. ex Willd.	TB	LAP 937
AMARYLLIDACEAE		
Bomarea sp.	OA	BKH 4713
ANACARDIACEAE		
Astronium urundeuva (Allemão) Engl.	SC	BKH 4760
Cardenasiodendron brachypterum (Loes) F. Barkley	TB	MS 1356
Schinus myrtifolius (Griseb.) Cabr.	OA, TB	BKH 4675; MS 1326
APIACEAE		
Eryngium ebracteatum Lam.	OA	BKH 4655
Eryngium elegans Cham.	OA	BKH 4674; 4711
Hydrocotyle humbodltii A. Rich.	TB	BKH 4622; MS 1287
APOCYNACEAE		
Forsteronia glabrescens Muell. Arg.	TB	MS 1438
Mandevilla laxa (Ruiz & Pav.) Woodson	TB	MS 1332
Prestonia sp.	TB	MS 1263

AQUIFOLIACEAE

Ilex argentina Lillo	TB	BKH 4601, 4673, 4876; MS 1358, 1429

ARACEAE

Gorgonidium mirabile Schott	TB	LAP 974
Philodendron undulatum Engler	SC	BKH 4953

ARALIACEAE

Oreopanax cf. *boliviensis* Seem.	TB	BKH 4615, 4638

ARECACEAE

Ceroxylon sp.	SC	BKH 4954

ASTERACEAE

sp. 1	TB	MS 1377
sp. 2	TB	BKH 4619
sp. 3	TB	LAP 969
Achyrocline latifolia Wedd.	OA	BKH 4665
Achyrocline satureioides (Lam.) DC.	OA	LAP 879
Aequatorium repandum (Wedd.) C. Jeffrey	TB	LAP 954
Ageratina azangaroensis (Sch.Bip. ex Wedd.) R. M. King & H. Rob.	OA	BKH 4715
Ageratina tenuis (R.E. Fries) R.M. King & H. Rob.	OA	BKH 4729; LAP 885
Antennaria linearifolia Wedd.	OA	BKH 4718
Baccharis chilco H.B.K.	OA	BKH 4742; LAP 878
Baccharis aff. *conwayii* Rusby	OA	BKH 4726
Baccharis dracunculifolia DC.	OA, SC	BKH 4716, 4777
Baccharis trimera DC.	OA	LAP 891
Bidens andicola H.B.K.	OA, TB	BKH 4717; MS 1327
Bidens pilosa L.	OA	BKH 4705
Bidens pseudocosmos Sherff	OA	LAP 900
Calea solidaginea H.B.K.	SC	BKH 4761
Chaptalia nutans (L.) Polak.	TB, OA	BKH 4626; LAP 903
Chromolaena connivens (Rusby) R.M. King & H. Rob.	OA	BKH 4653
Cnicothamnus lorentzii Griseb.	SC	BKH 4780
Conyza tunariensis (O. Kuntze) Zardini	OA	LAP 892

Critonia morifolia (Miller) R.M. King & H. Rob.	TB	MS 1414
Dasyphyllum brasiliense (Spreng.) Cabrera	TB	LAP 983
Dasyphyllum sp.	TB	BKH 4879
Elaphandra sp.	OA	LAP 896
Elephantopus mollis H.B.K.	SC	BKH 4779
Eupatorium bupleurifolium Hook. & Arn.	OA	BKH 4670
Hieracium adenocephalum (Sch.Bip.) Arv.-Touv.	OA	BKH 4730
Hypochoeris argentina Cabrera	OA	BKH 4710
Jungia pauciflora Rusby	TB	LAP 935
Jungia polita Griseb.	SC	BKH 4944
Kaunia lasiophthalma (Griseb.) R.M. King & H. Rob.	TB	LAP 924
Lepidaploa myriocephala (DC.) H. Rob.	TB	BKH 4827
Lepidaploa sp., immature	TB	BKH 4629
Lepidaploa tarijensis (Griseb.) H. Rob.	SC	BKH 4924
Mikania leucophylla (Rusby) B.L. Rob. var.?	TB	MS 1329
Mutisia campanulata Less.	TB	LAP 950; MS 1330
Ophyosporus piquerioides (DC.) Benth.	OA	BKH 4731
Ophyrosporus kuntzei Hieron.	OA	BKH 4734
Podocoma notobellidiastrum (Griseb.) G. L. Nesom	TB, OA	BKH 4644; MS 1291
Senecio alniphilus Cabrera	OA	BKH 4728
Senecio clivicolus Cabr.	OA	BKH 4704
Senecio epiphyticus O. Kuntze	TB	LAP 918, 953
Siegesbeckia jorullensis H.B.K.	OA	MS 1294
Stevia calderillensis Hieron.	OA	BKH 4735; LAP 886
Stevia fruticosa Griseb.	OA	BKH 4720
Stevia grisebachiana Hieron.	OA	BKH 4732
Stevia yaconensis Hieron.	OA	LAP 882
Tagetes ternifolia H.B.K.	OA	BKH 4712
Verbesina suncho (Griseb.) Blake	SC	BKH 4926
Vernonanthura ferruginea (Less.) H. Rob.	SC	BKH 4755
Vernonia sp.	SC	BKH 4923

BASELLACEAE

Anredera cordifolia (Tenore) Steenis	TB	MS 1270

BEGONIACEAE

Begonia juntasensis O. Kuntze	TB	MS 1373
Begonia micranthera Griseb.	TB	LAP 930

BERBERIDACEAE

Berberis fiebrigii C.K. Schneid.	OA	BKH 4687, 4725

BETULACEAE

Alnus acuminata H.B.K.	TB	BKH 4694; LAP 956; MS 1336

BIGNONIACEAE

sp.	TB	MS 1309
Amphilophium ? sp.	TB	MS 1442
Tabebuia cf. *chrysantha* (Jacq.) Nicholson	TB	LAP 1016
Tabebuia lapacho (K. Schum.) Sandw.	TB	MS 1304, 1360
Tabebuia sp.	SC	BKH 4754
Tecoma stans (L.) Juss. ex H.B.K.	SC	BKH 4748

BOMBACACEAE

Pseudobombax argentinum (R.E. Fries) Robyns	TB	MS 1420

BORAGINACEAE

Cordia alliodora (Ruiz & Pav.) Oken	SC, TB	BKH 4778, 4928; MS 1427
Patagonula americana L.	SC	BKH 4927

BRASSICACEAE

Cardamine africana L.	TB	LAP 926; MS 1393

BROMELIACEAE

sp.	OA	MS 1348
Aechmea distichantha Lem. var. *schlumbergeri* E. Morren ex Mez	SC	BKH 4948
Fosterella albicans (Griseb.) L.B. Sm.	TB	BKH 4837; MS 1409
Puya sp.	OA	BKH 4706
Tillandsia didisticha (E. Morren) Baker	SC	BKH 4768
Tillandsia duratii Visiana	SC	BKH 4769
Tillandsia loliacea Mart. ex Schult. f.	SC	BKH 4764, 4956
Tillandsia sp.	TB	BKH 4823
Tillandsia sp.	TB	LAP 960
Tillandsia tenuifolia L.	SC	BKH 4770

Tillandsia tricholepis Baker	SC	BKH 4765
Tillandsia usneoides (L.) L.	SC, TB	BKH 4783, 4843
Vriesea friburgensis Mez	SC	BKH 4887
Vriesea maxoniana (L.B. Sm.) L.B. Sm.	TB	BKH 4801
CACTACEAE		
Cleistocactus sp.	SC	BKH 4955
Discocactus ramulosus (Salm-Dyck) Kimnach	SC	BKH 4794
Rhipsalis tucumanensis F.A.C. Weber	TB	MS 1275
CAESALPINIACEAE		
Bauhinia longicuspus Spruce ex Benth.	SC	BKH 4885
Caesalpinia floribunda Tul.	SC	BKH 4947
Pterogyne nitens Tul.	SC	BKH 4749
Senna hirsuta H.S. Irwin & Barneby	TB	LAP 977
Senna mandonii (Benth.) H.S. Irwin & Barneby	OA	BKH 4671
Senna aff. *rugosa* (G. Don) H.S. Irwin & Barneby	SC	BKH 4766
Senna spectabilis (DC.) H.S. Irwin & Barneby	TB	LAP 1005
CAMPANULACEAE		
Lobelia xalapensis H.B.K.	TB	MS 1395
Siphocampylus orbignianus A. DC.	TB	LAP 970
Siphocampylus tupaeformis Zahlbr.	OA	BKH 4733
CANNACEAE		
Canna indica L.	TB	MS 1334
CAPPARIDACEAE		
Capparis prissea Macbr., s. l.	SC	BKH 4812
CAPRIFOLIACEAE		
Sambucus peruviana H.B.K.	TB	MS 1376
Viburnum seemenii Graebn.	OA, TB	BKH 4603; LAP 884; MS 1266
CARYOPHYLLACEAE		
Drymaria ovata Humb. & Bonpl. ex Roem. & Schult.	OA	LAP 902
Drymaria sp.	SC	BKH 4904
CELASTRACEAE		
Maytenus ilicifolia Reiss.	SC	BKH 4781

Schaefferia argentinensis Speg.	SC	BKH 4918
CLETHRACEAE		
Clethra scabra Pers.	TB	BKH 4602, 4640; LAP 1015
Clethra aff. *scabra* Pers.	TB	LAP 1007
CLUSIACEAE		
Hypericum silenoides Juss.	OA	BKH 4688
COLUMELLIACEAE		
Columellia oblonga Ruiz & Pav.	OA, TB	BKH 4701, 4740
COMBRETACEAE		
Terminalia triflora (Griseb.) Lillo	TB	BKH 4608; LAP 1018; MS 1367, 1441
COMMELINACEAE		
Callisia monandra (Sw.) J.H. Schult.	SC	BKH 4790
Tradescantia sp.	TB	LAP 945
CONVOLVULACEAE		
Cuscuta odorata Ruiz & Pav.	TB	MS 1289
Evolvulus latifolius Ker.-Gawl.	TB	MS 1418
CRASSULACEAE		
sp.	OA	MS 1372
CYPERACEAE		
Bulbostylis sphaerocephala (Boeck.) C.B. Clarke	OA	BKH 4689
Cyperus laxus Lam.	OA	BKH 4819
Rhynchospora sp.	TB	BKH 4621; MS 1264, 1278
Scleria latifolia Sw.	TB	MS 1396
DIOSCOREACEAE		
Dioscorea chiquiacensis Kunth	OA	MS 1292
Dioscorea larecajensis Uline ex Kunth	OA	BKH 4743
Dioscorea sp.	SC	BKH 4886
DROSERACEAE		
Drosera villosa A. St.-Hil.	OA	BKH 4700; LAP 965
ELAEOCARPACEAE		
Crinodendron tucumanum Lillo	TB	LAP 929, 943
Muntingia calabura ? L.	TB	MS 1423

Vallea stipularis L. f.	TB	BKH 4646, 4883; MS 1302
ERICACEAE		
Agarista boliviensis (Sleumer) Judd	TB	BKH 4871
Bejaria aestuans L.	TB	BKH 4632, 4695
Gaultheria vaccinioides Wedd.	OA	BKH 4648; LAP 883
ERYTHROXYLACEAE		
Erythroxylum cuneifolium (Mart.) O. Schulz	SC	BKH 4940
EUPHORBIACEAE		
Croton quadrisetosus Lam.	TB	MS 1362
Croton saltensis Griseb.	SC	BKH 4802
Croton aff. *saltensis* Griseb.	TB	BKH 4880
Croton urucurana Baill.	TB	MS 1434
Croton sp.	TB	BKH 4881
Euphorbia acerensis Boiss.	SC	BKH 4789
Euphorbia portulacoides L.	OA	BKH 4719
Phyllanthus niuri L.	OA	MS 1339
Tragia volubilis L.	TB	BKH 4872
FABACEAE		
Collaea speciosa (Lois.) DC.	OA	BKH 4660
Crotalaria stipularia Desv.	OA	BKH 4669
Dalbergia ? sp.	TB	BKH 4831
Desmodium sp.	OA	BKH 4686
Desmodium uncinatum (Jacq.) DC.	OA	LAP 895
Erythrina falcata Benth.	SC	BKH 4951
Lonchocarpus lilloi (Hassler) Burkart	TB	LAP 995
Lupinus celsimontanus C.P. Smith	OA	BKH 4741
Myroxylon peruiferum L. f.	TB	BKH 4832; MS 1426
Rhynchosia naineckensis Fortunato	SC, TB	BKH 4809; MS 1416
Tipuana tipu (Benth.) O. Kuntze	TB	MS 1422, 1431, 1439
Vigna luteola (Jay) Benth.	OA	BKH 4663
FLACOURTIACEAE		
Casearia sylvestris Sw.	TB	LAP 1011
GENTIANACEAE		
Gentianella bicolor (Wedd.) Fabris	OA	BKH 4693

Gentianella kuntzii Gilg	OA	BKH 4652
Gentianella silenoides (Gilg) Fabris	OA	BKH 4703
Voyria flavescens Griseb.	TB	LAP 1017
GERANIACEAE		
Geranium aff. *fallax* Steud.	OA	BKH 4709
Geranium pflanzii R. Knuth	OA	BKH 4714
GESNERIACEAE		
Seemania gymnostoma (Griseb.) Tours.	SC	BKH 4763, 4933
GUNNERACEAE		
Gunnera apiculata Schindl.	TB	BKH 4747
HIPPOCRATEACEAE		
Pristimera andina Miers	SC	BKH 4929
ICACINACEAE		
Citronella apogon (Griseb.) R.A. Howard	TB	LAP 990; MS 1430
IRIDACEAE		
Sisyrinchium alatum Hook.	OA	BKH 4672
Sisyrinchium sp.1	TB	MS 1300
Sisyrinchium sp. 2	OA	BKH 4657
JUGLANDACEAE		
Juglans australis Griseb.	TB	MS 1392
JUNCACEAE		
Juncus tenuis Willd.	OA	BKH 4722
Luzula excelsa Buchenau	OA	BKH 4721
LAMIACEAE		
Hyptis mutabilis (Rich.) Briq.	SC, OA	BKH 4920; LAP 897
Hyptis suaveolens (L.) Poit.	SC	BKH 4917
Lepechinia graveolens (Regel) Epling	OA	LAP 899
Salvia personata Epling	TB	MS 1370
Scutellaria purpurascens Sw.	SC	BKH 4919
LAURACEAE		
sp. 1	TB	BKH 4848
sp. 2	TB	BKH 4859
Nectandra angusta Rohwer	TB	LAP 1002; MS 1405
Ocotea sp. 1	TB	LAP 968

Ocotea sp. 2	TB	BKH 4607; LAP 967, 1021
Ocotea sp. 3	TB	BKH 4835, 4849
Persea sp. 1	TB	BKH 4641; LAP 948; MS 1312, 1387
Persea sp. 2	TB	BKH 4618; MS 1355
Phoebe porphyria (Griseb.) Mez	TB	BKH 4845; MS 1350, 1354, 1365
Phoebe cf. *porphyria* (Griseb.) Mez	TB	LAP 1010; MS 1413
LILIACEAE		
Cordyline sp.	TB	BKH 4869
LINACEAE		
Linum filiforme Urb.	OA	BKH 4746
LOGANIACEAE		
Spigelia rojasiana Kraenzl.	TB	BKH 4864
LORANTHACEAE		
Phoradendron tucumanense Urb.	TB	MS 1440
LYTHRACEAE		
Cuphea calophylla (Koehne) Lourteig	OA	BKH 4702
Cuphea racemosa (L. f.) Spreng.	OA	BKH 4818
Cuphea scaberrima Koehne	OA	LAP 881
MALVACEAE		
Pavonia cf. *eurychlamys* Ulrich	OA	LAP 901
Pavonia sepium St. Hil.	SC	BKH 4943
Sida aff. *glabra* Mill.	SC	BKH 4921
Sida rhombifolia L.	OA	MS 1284
Tarasa capitata (Cav.) D. Bates	OA	BKH 4708
Wissadula densiflora R.E. Fries	SC	BKH 4931
MARANTACEAE		
Stromanthe sp.	TB	MS 1436
MELASTOMATACEAE		
Miconia calvescens DC.	TB	LAP 978, 1008; MS 1433
Miconia cyanocarpa Naud.	TB	MS 1262
Tibouchina cf. *alpestris* Cogn.	TB, OA	BKH 4628, 4639; LAP 907
Tibouchina herzogii Cogn. ex char.	OA	LAP 894

Tibouchina or *Brachyotum*	TB	LAP 963
MELIACEAE		
Cedrela lilloi C. DC	TB	LAP 949; MS 1295, 1406
Trichilia clausseni C. DC.	SC, TB	BKH 4806; LAP 992
MIMOSACEAE		
Acacia aroma Gillies ex Hook. & Arn.	SC	BKH 4767
Anadenanthera macrocarpa (Benth.) Brenan	SC	BKH 4937
Enterolobium contortisilquum (Well) Morong.	TB	LAP 994
Inga marginata Willd.	TB	BKH 4833; LAP 1003
Inga saltensis Burkart	TB	BKH 4840; MS 1361
Mimosa lepidota Herzog	OA	BKH 4738
Mimosa xanthocentra Mart.	SC	BKH 4762
Parapiptadenia excelsa (Griseb.) Baker	TB	BKH 4614; MS 1386
Pithecellobium scarale Griseb.	SC	BKH 4757
Pithecellobium sp.	TB	BKH 4617; MS 1281
MORACEAE		
Ficus guaranitica Chodat	TB	MS 1402
Maclura tinctoria (L.) Steud.	TB	LAP 993
MYRICACEAE		
Myrica pubescens Humb. & Bonpl. ex Willd.	TB	BKH 4737
MYRSINACEAE		
Myrsine coriacea (Sw.) R. Br. ex Roem. & Schult.	OA, SC, TB	BKH 4759, 4616; LAP 880
Myrsine sp.	TB	MS 1307
MYRTACEAE		
Amomytrella guili (Speg.) Kausel	OA, TB	LAP 910, 911; MS 1333
Blepharocalyx salicifolius (H.B.K.) O. Berg	TB	MS 1349, 1379
cf. *Calycorectes psidiiflorus* (O. Berg) Sobral	SC, TB	BKH 4771, 4909; MS 1390
Eugenia cf. *feijoi* O. Berg	TB	BKH 4836
Eugenia uniflora L.	SC	BKH 4908
Myrcia cf. *multiflora* (Lam.) DC.	TB	BKH 4613; MS 1359, 1369, 1380, 1383
Myrcia sp. 1	TB	BKH 4853; MS 1352
Myrcianthes cf. *callicoma* McVaugh	TB	BKH 4604; MS 1368
Myrcianthes pseudomato (Legrand) McVaugh	TB	BKH 4609, 4862; MS 1351

Myrcianthes pungens (O. Berg) Legrand	SC	BKH 4907
Myrciaria cf. *floribunda* (West ex Willd.) O. Berg	TB	LAP 1006
Myrciaria sp.	SC	BKH 4772
Psidium guajava L.	SC	BKH 4752
Psidium guineense Sw.	SC	BKH 4750, 4751
Siphoneugena occidentalis Legrand	TB	BKH 4606; LAP 981, 1009, 1014; MS 1310, 1394

NYCTAGINACEAE

Pisonia ambigua Heimerl	TB	BKH 4846; LAP 991; MS 1410

OLACACEAE

Ximenia americana L.	TB	MS 1424

ONAGRACEAE

Fuchsia boliviana Carrière	OA, TB	BKH 4631; MS 1338

ORCHIDACEAE

sp. 1	SC	BKH 4791
sp. 2	TB	BKH 4884
Campylocentrum fasciola (Lindl.) Cogn.	TB	MS 1375
Capanemia sp.	OA	BKH 4685
Cranichis sp.	SC	BKH 4773, 4785
Cyclopogon sp.	SC	BKH 4902
Cyrtopodium sp.	TB	BKH 4828
Encyclia pflanzii Schltr.	SC, TB	BKH 4914; MS 1421
Encyclia sp.	SC	BKH 4799, 4898
Habenaria pumiloides C. Schum.	OA	BKH 4745
Habenaria sp.	SC	BKH 4797
Isochilus linearis (Jacq.) R. Br.	SC	BKH 4798, 4913
Liparis nervosa (Thun.) Lindl.	SC	BKH 4784
Malaxis sp.	TB	BKH 4684; LAP 933
Palmorchis sp.	TB	LAP 986
Pleurothallis obovata (Lindl.) Lindl.	SC	BKH 4912
Pleurothallis pubescens Lindl.	SC	BKH 4895, 4911
Pleurothallis sp.	TB	BKH 4826
Polystachya foliosa (Hook.) Rchb. f.	SC	BKH 4906, 4915
Sarcoglottis sp.	SC	BKH 4815

Stanhopea sp.	SC	BKH 4896
OXALIDACEAE		
Oxalis mollissima (Rusby) Kunth	OA, SC, TB	BKH 4903, 4673; LAP 906
PAPAVERACEAE		
Bocconia pearcei Hutch.	TB	LAP 975
PASSIFLORACEAE		
Passiflora naviculata Griseb.	OA	BKH 4744
Passiflora tenuifolia Killip	TB	MS 1407
PHYTOLACCACEAE		
Petiveria alliacea L.	SC, TB	BKH 4805, 4824
Phytolacca bogotensis H.B.K.	TB	BKH 4878
PIPERACEAE		
Peperomia alata Yuncker	SC	BKH 4808
Peperomia blanda (Jacq.) H.B.K.	SC, TB	BKH 4788, 4636, 4642
Peperomia cf. *cardenasii* Trel.	TB	MS 1343
Peperomia hispidula (Sw.) A. Dietr.	TB	LAP 939
Peperomia silvarum C. DC.	OA, TB	BKH 4667, 4841; LAP 887
Peperomia sp. 1	TB	LAP 942
Peperomia sp. 2	TB	MS 1301
Peperomia theodori Trel.	SC	BKH 4800
Peperomia aff. *tominiana* C. DC.	TB	LAP 928; MS 1311
Piper aff. *amalago* L.	TB	LAP 944
Piper hieronymi C. DC.	TB	BKH 4856; LAP 989; MS 1347
Piper tucumanum C. DC.	TB	LAP 971, 998; MS 1391
PLANTAGINACEAE		
Plantago australis Lam.	OA, TB	BKH 4692; MS 1282, 1401
POACEAE		
sp.	SC	BKH 4939
Aulonemia sp.	TB	BKH 4839
Axonopus barbigerus (Kunth.) Hitchc.	OA	BKH 4691
Axonopus compressus (Sw.) P. Beauv.	OA	BKH 4661
Axonopus siccus (Nees) Kuhlm.	OA	BKH 4690
Calamagrostis sp.	OA	BKH 4658, 4724
Chusquea sp.	TB	BKH 4625

Homolepis glutinosa (Sw.) Zuloaga & Soder.	TB, OA	BKH 4865; LAP 905
Ichnanthus pallens (Sw.) Munro ex Benth.	TB	MS 1404
Ichnanthus tenuis (J. Presl) Hitchc. & Chase	TB	BKH 4877; MS 1397
Lamprothyrsus sp.	OA	MS 1337
Lasiacis divaricata Davidse	TB	MS 1437
Olyra fasciculata Trin.	TB	MS 1415
Panicum sp.	TB	BKH 4623
Panicum trichoides Sw.	SC	BKH 4938
Paspalum mandiocum Trin.	TB	MS 1398
Schizachyrium microstachyum (Desv.) Roseng. et al.	SC, OA	BKH 4650, 4936
Schizachyrium sanguineum (Retz.) Alston	SC	BKH 4949
Setaria vulpiseta (Lam.) Hitchc. & Chase	SC	BKH 4934
Stipa ichu (Ruiz & Pav.) Kunth	OA	BKH 4723
PODOCARPACEAE		
Podocarpus parlatorei Pilger	TB	LAP 955
POLYGALACEAE		
Monnina conferta Ruiz & Pav.	OA	LAP 909
POLYGONACEAE		
Muehlenbeckia tamnifolia (H.B.K.) Meissn.	OA	BKH 4727
Polygonum punctatum Elliot	OA	BKH 4817
PROTEACEAE		
Roupala meisneri Sleumer	TB	BKH 4611; MS 1357, 1374
RANNUNCULACEAE		
Clematis sericea H.B.K. ex DC.	TB	LAP 982
Thalictrum sp.	OA	BKH 4678
RHAMNACEAE		
Rhamnus sphaerosperma Sw.	TB	BKH 4612
ROSACEAE		
Polylepis hieronymi Pilger	TB	BKH 4651, 4739
Prunus integrifolia (C. Presl) Walp.	TB	LAP 1012, 1013
Prunus tucumanensis Lillo	TB	BKH 4610
Rubus boliviensis Focke	TB	MS 1293
RUBIACEAE		
Coccocypselum lanceolatum (Ruiz & Pav.) Pers.	OA	BKH 4656; LAP 908

Coutarea hexandra K. Schum.	SC	BKH 4946
Galium hypocarpium (L.) Griseb.	OA	BKH 4659, 4662
Hamelia patens Jacq.	SC	BKH 4941
Manettia cordifolia Mart.	SC, TB	BKH 4901, 4830
Nertera granadensis (L. f.) Druce	OA	BKH 4736
Palicourea sp.	TB	BKH 4852
Pogonopus tubulosus (DC.) K. Schum.	TB	observed
Psychotria cf. *alba* Ruiz & Pav.	TB	BKH 4857; MS 1417
Psychotria yungasensis Rusby	TB	BKH 4624; MS 1261, 1344
Randia cf. *armata* (Sw.) DC.	TB	MS 1381
Randia sp.	OA	MS 1308
RUTACEAE		
Citrus aurantium L.	TB	LAP 999
Fagara pterota L.	SC	BKH 4932
Zanthoxylum naranjillo (Griseb.) Engl.	SC, TB	BKH 4811; MS 1432
Zanthoxylum rhoifolia (Lam.) Engl.	SC	BKH 4950
SAPINDACEAE		
Allophylus edulis (St.-Hil., Cambess. & Juss.) Radlk.	TB	BKH 4868; MS 1303, 1353
Cardiospermum corindum L.	TB	LAP 951
Cupania vernalis Cambess.	TB	BKH 4858; LAP 873; MS 1298, 1363
Diatenopterix sorbifolia Radlk.	TB	LAP 1020; MS 1412, 1435
Dilodendron bipinnatum Radlk.	SC	BKH 4756
Dodonaea viscosa (L.) Jacq.	TB	LAP 876
Serjania sufferruginea Radlk.	TB	LAP 985
Thinouia sp.	TB	LAP 987
SAPOTACEAE		
Chrysophyllum gonocarpum (Mart. & Eichl.) Engl.	TB	BKH 4847; LAP 984, 997; MS 1403
SAXIFRAGACEAE		
Escallonia hypoglauca Herzog	OA, TB	BKH 4649; LAP 904, 1962
SCROPHULARIACEAE		
Agalinus genistifolia (Cham. & Schltdl.) D'Arcy	OA	LAP 893

SOLANACEAE

sp.	TB	LAP 947
Brunfelsia ? australis Benth.	TB	LAP 932
Cestrum strigilatum Ruiz & Pav.	TB	BKH 4854
Solanum americanum Mill.	TB	MS 1305
Solanum aff. *glaucophyllum* Dunal	TB	LAP 931; MS 1299, 1385
Solanum pseudocapsicum L.	SC	BKH 4945
Solanum schlechtendalianum Walp.	TB	LAP 976
Solanum sp. 1	TB	BKH 4850; LAP 874
Solanum sp. 2	SC	BKH 4753
Solanum sp. 3	TB	MS 1382
Solanum sp. 4	TB	LAP 946
Solanum sp. 5	TB	BKH 4645

STAPHYLEACEAE

Turpinia cf. *occidentalis* (Sw.) G. Don	TB	LAP 996
Ayenia odonellii Cristóbal	SC	BKH 4942

STERCULIACEAE

Byttneria catalpaefolia Jacq.	TB	BKH 4825

STYRACACEAE

Styrax argenteus J.S. Presl	TB	BKH 4863; LAP 934

SYMPLOCACEAE

Symplocos aff. *subcuneata* (Herzog) Ståll	TB	BKH 4605, 4676

TILIACEAE

Heliocarpus americanus L.	TB	MS 1411
Luehea fiebrigii Burret	TB	LAP 979; MS 1425
Triumfetta semitriloba Jacq.	SC	BKH 4935

TROPAEOLACEAE

Tropaeolum meyeri Sparre	TB	LAP 872

ULMACEAE

Celtis iguanaea (Jacq.) Sarg.	TB	BKH 4855; MS 1371

URTICACEAE

Boehmeria caudata Sw.	TB	LAP 921; MS 1296, 1340
Boehmeria cylindrica (L.) Sw.	TB	MS 1399

Phenax laevigatus Wedd.	TB	MS 1328
Pilea dauciodora Wedd.	TB	LAP 920
Urera altissima Lillo	TB	BKH 4866; LAP 877
Urera caracasana (Jacq.) Steudel	TB	LAP 1004
VERBENACEAE		
Aegiphila saltensis Legname	TB	LAP 875; MS 1364, 1378, 1428
Duranta serratifolia (Griseb.) Kuntze	TB	LAP 922; MS 1331, 1384
Lantana micrantha Briq.	SC	BKH 4930
Verbena intermedia Gillies & Hook.	TB	MS 1400
VIOLACEAE		
Rinorea sp.	TB	BKH 4838
VITACEAE		
Cissus cf. *lanceolata* Malme	TB	MS 1335
VOCHYSIACEAE		
Qualea sp.	SC	BKH 4758
PTERIDOPHYTA		
Adiantopsis chlorophylla (Sw.) Fée	SC, TB	BKH 4952; LAP 972
Adiantopsis radiata (L.) Fée	SC, TB	BKH 4803; LAP 867
Adiantum pectinatum Kunze ex Baker	TB	BKH 4829
Adiantum raddianum C. Presl	SC, TB	BKH 4787; LAP 866
Alsophila incana (H. Karst.) D.S. Conant? sterile	TB	MS 1274
Anemia ferruginea Kunth var. *ferruginea*	OA	BKH 4668
Anemia phyllitidis (L.) Sw.	SC, TB	BKH 4810; LAP 870
Asplenium vel aff. *argentinum* Hieron.	SC, TB	BKH 4804; LAP 868, 927, 019; MS 1268
Asplenium formosum Willd.	SC	BKH 4786
Asplenium inaequilaterale Willd.	TB	LAP 869
Asplenium pumilum Sw.	TB	LAP 865
Asplenium rigidum Sw.	TB	MS 1267
Asplenium serra Langsd. & Fisch.	TB	BKH 4860; LAP 914
Asplenium sp.	OA	BKH 4821
Blechnum glandulosum Link	OA, TB	BKH 4627; LAP 890; MS 1265

Blechnum lanceola Sw.	OA	BKH 4822
Blechnum occidentale L.	SC	BKH 4796
Blechnum penna-marina (Poiret) Kuhn	TB	LAP 964
Blechnum schomburgkii (Klotzsch) C. Chr.	OA	BKH 4699
Blechnum sp. (sterile and perhaps juvenile)	TB	BKH 4630
Blechnum sprucei C. Chr.	TB, OA	LAP 913; MS 1269
Bolbitis serratifolia (M. Martens ex Kaulf.) Schott	SC	BKH 4795
Campyloneurum aglaolepis (Alston) de la Sota	TB	LAP 871; MS 1276
Campyloneurum pascoense R.M. Tryon & A.F. Tryon	TB	LAP 915
Cheilanthes poeppigiana Mett. ex Kuhn	OA	BKH 4677
Cheilanthes squamosa (Gill ex Hook. & Grev.) Lowe	OA	LAP 889
Diplazium lilloi (Hicken) R.M. Tryon & A.F. Tryon	TB	LAP 936
Doryopteris concolor (Langsd. & Fisch.) Kuhn	SC	BKH 4792, 4892
Doryopteris crenulans (Fée) H. Christ	OA, TB	BKH 4697, 4874; LAP 966
Doryopteris lorentzii (Hieron.) Diels	TB	LAP 864
Doryopteris nobilis (T. Moore) C. Chr.	TB	LAP 1000
Doryopteris pedata (L.) Fée var. *multipartita* (Fée) Tryon	TB	MS 1366
Dryopteris wallichiana (Spreng.) Hyl.	OA, TB	LAP 912; MS 1288, 1389
Elaphoglossum cuspidatum (Willd.) T. Moore	OA	BKH 4666, 4696
Elaphoglossum aff. *erinaceum* (Fée) T. Moore	TB	LAP 917
Elaphoglossum piloselloides (C. Presl) T. Moore	OA	MS 1341
Elaphoglossum sp. 1	TB	BKH 4851
Elaphoglossum sp. 2	TB	BKH 4861
Elaphoglossum sp. 3	OA	MS 1280, 1297
Equisetum bogotense Kunth	OA	BKH 4816
Hemionitis tomentosa (Lam.) Raddi	SC	BKH 4807, 4899
Huperzia sp., aff. *hartwegiana* (Spring) Trev.	OA	MS 1279
Hymenophyllum capurroi de la Sota	TB	LAP 941
Hymenophyllum crispum Kunth	TB	LAP 940
Hymenophyllum polyanthos (Sw.) Sw.	TB	BKH 4643, 4867; MS 1286
Lastreopsis effusa (Sw.) Tindale	TB	LAP 988

Lellingeria obovata (Copel.) A.R. Sm. & R.C. Moran	OA	MS 1345
Lycopodium clavatum L.	OA, TB	BKH 4654, 4875; MS 1283
Lycopodium thyoides Humb. & Bonpl. ex Willd.	OA, TB	BKH 4647, 4873; LAP 888
Melpomene peruviana (Desv.) A.R. Sm. & R.C. Moran	OA	BKH 4698
Microgramma squamulosa (Kaulf.) de la Sota	OA	MS 1277
Pecluma eurybasis var. *glabrescens* (Rosenst.) Lellinger	OA	MS 1271
Pleopeltis macrocarpa (Bory ex Willd.) Kaulf.	TB	LAP 961
Polypodium latipes Langsd. & Fisch.	TB	BKH 4635; LAP 923; MS 1272
Polypodium pseudoaureum Cav.	SC	BKH 4813
Polypodium sp. (undescribed?)	OA	MS 1273
Polystichum nudicaule Rosenst.	TB	BKH 4620, 4634
Pteridium arachnoideum (Kaulf.) Maxon	TB	LAP 980
Pteris deflexa Link	TB	BKH 4633; LAP 925; MS 1306, 1419
Pteris denticulata Sw.	SC	BKH 4900
Selaginella novae-hollandiae (Sw.) Spring	OA, TB	BKH 4683, 4774, 4894; MS 1321, 1346
Selaginella sulcata Spring ex Mart.	SC	BKH 4775, 4776, 4782, 4905
Thelypteris (*Amauropelta*) cf. *jujuyensis* de la Sota	OA	MS 1285
Thelypteris hispidula (Decne.) C.F. Reed	OA	BKH 4820
Thelypteris patens (Sw.) Small var. *smithiana* Ponce	SC	BKH 4814
Trichomanes angustatum Carm.	TB	LAP 938, 952
BRYOPHYTA		
sp.	TB	BKH 4681
sp.	TB	BKH 4680
sp.	TB	BKH 4679
sp.	SC	BKH 4897
sp.	SC	BKH 4910
sp.	TB	BKH 4682

sp.	TB	MS 1319
Campylopus fragilis (Brid.) Bruch & Schimp.	TB	LAP 959
Chrysohypnum elegantulum (Hook.) Hampe	TB	MS 1408
Entodon beyrichii (Schwägr.) C. Mull.	SC	BKH 4888
Entodon hampeanus C. Mull.	TB	LAP 1001
Holomitrium crispulum Mitt.	TB	MS 1313, 1324
Leucobryum crispum Mart.	TB	BKH 4844
Macromitium punctatum (Hook & Grev.) Brid.	TB	MS 1314
Pilotrichella pentasticha (Brid.) Wisk & Marq.	SC, TB	BKH 4889, 4870; MS 1318
Plagiomnium rhynchophorum (Hook.) R. Kep.	SC	BKH 4916
Polytrichum juniperinum Hedw.	TB	MS 1325
Porotrichum filiferum Mitt.	SC	BKH 4890, 4891
Rhaphidorrhynchium capillifolium (Herz.) Broth.	TB	MS 1317
Rhodobryum beyrichianum (Hor.) Mull. ex Ham.	TB	LAP 957
Thurdium delicatulum (Hedw.) B.S.G.	TB	BKH 4882
Bryophyta ?	TB	MS 1320

Plant Transect Data from the Río Urucuti Basin, South Central Chuquisaca, Bolivia

Bruce K. Holst, Martha Serrano, and Luzmilla Arroyo Padilla

All transects: 100 trees counted. Bolivia, Dept. Chuquisaca, Provincia Sud Cinti.

Transect 1 - 88 x 10 m

13 May 1995. Aprox. 300 m north of Rinconada del Bufete Camp (20°49'49"S, 64°22'28"W), near the base of the northern wall of Cerro Bufete. 2050 m elevation. Low (5-10 m tall) semi-evergreen cloud forest on ridge top.

Family	Genus, species	Number of individuals >10 cm dbh in transect	Number of trees >30 cm dbh in transect (in parentheses)
Caprifoliaceae	*Viburnum seemenii*	41	
Aquifoliaceae	*Ilex argentina*	27	
Clethraceae	*Clethra scabra*	17	
Lauraceae	*Ocotea* sp. 2	4	
Symplocaceae	*Symplocos* aff. *subcuneata*	3	
Rosaceae	*Prunus tucumanensis*	2	
Combretaceae	*Terminalia triflora*	1	
Myrtaceae	?	1	
Myrtaceae	*Myrcianthes* cf. *callicoma*	1	
Myrtaceae	*Myrcianthes pseudomato*	1	
Myrtaceae	*Siphoneugena occidentalis*	1	
Proteaceae	*Roupala meisneri*	1	

Transect 2 - 120 x 10 m

15 May 1995. Northeastern base of Cerro Bufete, ca. 200 m east of Rinconada del Bufete camp (20°49'49"S, 64°22'28"W). 2000 m elevation. Tall (20-30 m) semi-evergreen, mossy cloudforest on rocky slope.

Family	Genus, species	Number of individuals >10 cm dbh in transect	Number of trees >30 cm dbh in transect (in parentheses)
Myrtaceae	*Siphoneugena occidentalis*	53	(4)
Pteridophyta	*Alsophila incana* (sterile)	21	
Caprifoliaceae	*Viburnum seemenii*	5	
Elaeocarpaceae	*Crinodendron tucumanum*	4	(2)
Lauraceae	*Persea* sp. 1	4	(4)
Meliaceae	*Cedrela lilloi*	3	(2)
Euphorbiaceae	*Croton* sp.	2	
Aquifoliaceae	*Ilex argentina*	1	(1)
Araliaceae	*Oreopanax* cf. *boliviensis*	1	
Clethraceae	*Clethra scabra*	1	
Myrsinaceae	*Myrsine coriacea*	1	
Styracaceae	*Styrax argenteus*	1	

Transect 3 - 116 x 10 m

18 May 1995. Immediately north of Río Limonal. 20°49'41"S, 64°22'37"W, 1850 m elevation. Tall (20-25 m) semi-evergeen cloudforest on steep, rocky slope.

Family	Genus, species	Number of individuals >10 cm dbh in transect	Number of trees >30 cm dbh in transect (in parentheses)
Verbenaceae	*Aegiphila saltensis*	31	
Lauraceae	*Phoebe porphyria*	10	(2)
Sapindaceae	*Allophyllus edulis*	10	
?		7	(7)
Sapindaceae	*Cupania vernalis*	7	
Aquifoliaceae	*Ilex argentina*	4	(2)
Euphorbiaceae	*Croton quadrisetosus*	4	
Proteaceae	*Roupala meisneri*	4	
Lauraceae	*Persea* sp.	3	(1)
Myrtaceae	*Myrcianthes pseudomato*	3	
Myrtaceae	*Myrcianthes rhopaloides?*	3	
Anacardiaceae	*Cardenasiodendron brachypterum*	2	(2)
Caprifoliaceae	*Viburnum seemenii*	2	
Mimosaceae	*Inga saltensis*	2	
Myrsinaceae	*Myrsine coriacea*	2	
Myrtaceae	*Myrcia* cf. *multiflora*	2	
Araliaceae	*Oreopanax* cf. *boliviensis*	1	
Bignoniaceae	*Tabebuia lapacho*	1	
Mimosaceae	*Parapiptadenia excelsa*	1	(1)
Myrtaceae	*Blepharocalyx salicifolius*	1	(1)

Transect 4 - 114 x 10 m

20 May 1995. Aprox. 500 m north of Rinconada del Bufete Camp (20°49'49"S, 64°22'28"W), near the northern base of Cerro Bufete. 2040 m elevation. Tall (20-30 m) semi-evergreen cloudforest on gentle slope.

Family	Genus, species	Number of individuals >10 cm dbh in transect	Number of trees >30 cm dbh in transect (in parentheses)
Myrtaceae	*Myrcianthes pseudomato*	18	(2)
Myrtaceae	*Myrcia* cf. *multiflora*	17	
Myrtaceae	*Blepharocalyx salicifolius*	12	(5)
Aquifoliaceae	*Ilex argentina*	10	(3)
Caprifoliaceae	*Viburnum seemenii*	8	
Rosaceae	*Prunus tucumanensis*	5	(1)
Sapindaceae	*Allophyllus edulis*	5	
Verbenaceae	*Aegiphila saltensis*	5	
Verbenaceae	*Duranta serratifolia*	5	
Lauraceae	*Persea* sp. 1	4	(4)
Araliaceae	*Oreopanax* cf. *boliviensis*	3	(1)
Mimosaceae	*Parapiptadenia excelsa*	3	(3)
Meliaceae	*Cedrela lilloi*	2	(2)
Myrtaceae	*Myrcianthes rhopaloides* ?	2	(2)
Lauraceae		1	(1)

Transect 5 - 117 x 10 m

26 May 1995. Río Santa Martha, El Limón camp. 20°42'41"S, 64°18'19"W. 950 m elevation. Tall (20-25 m) semi-evergreen forest on alluvial valley bottom.

Family	Genus, species	Number of individuals >10 cm dbh in transect	Number of trees >30 cm dbh in transect (in parentheses)
Rutaceae	*Citrus aurantium*	45	
Piperaceae	*Piper tucumanensis*	15	
Lauraceae	*Nectandra angusta*	10	(1)
Mimosaceae	*Inga marginata*	7	(1)
Icacinaceae	*Citronella apogon*	4	(1)
Fabaceae	*Lonchocarpus lilloi*	3	(2)
Sapotaceae	*Chrysophyllum gonocarpum*	3	(1)
Meliaceae	*Cedrela lilloi*	2	(1)
Mimosaceae	*Enterolobium contortisiliquum*	2	(1)
Nyctaginaceae	*Pisonia ambigua*	2	
Bignoniaceae	*Tabebuia lapacho*	1	(1)
Caesalpiniaceae	*Senna spectabilis*	1	(1)
Meliaceae	*Trichilia clausseni*	1	
Moraceae	*Maclura tinctoria*	1	
Myrtaceae	*Siphoneugena occidentalis*	1	
Staphyleaceae	*Turpinia occidentalis*	1	
Urticaceae	*Urera caracasana*	1	

Transect 6 - 120 x 10 m

26 May 1995. First ridge to the north of Río Santa Martha. 20°42'41"S, 64°18'19"W. 1000-1050 m elevation. Tall (25 m) semi-evergreen forest on undulating hills.

Family	Genus, species	Number of individuals >10 cm dbh in transect	Number of trees >30 cm dbh in transect (in parentheses)
Myrtaceae	*Siphoneugena* occidentalis	38	(6)
Rosaceae	*Prunus integrifolia*	15	(3)
Myrtaceae	*Myrciaria* cf. *floribunda*	12	
Bignoniaceae	*Tabebuia* cf. *chrysantha*	8	
Proteaceae	*Roupala* montana	7	(1)
Clethraceae	*Clethra* aff. *scabra*	4	
Clethraceae	*Clethra* scabra	2	(1)
Meliaceae	*Cedrela lilloi*	2	
Meliaceae	*Trichilia clausseni*	2	
Sapindaceae	*Cupania vernalis* Camb.	2	
Sapindaceae	*Diatenopterix sorbifolia*	1	
Combretaceae	*Terminalia triflora*	1	
Flacourtiaceae	*Casearia sylvestris*	1	
Lauraceae	*Ocotea* sp. 2	1	
Lauraceae	*Phoebe* cf. *porphyria*	1	
Melastomataceae	*Miconia calvescens*, probably	1	
Rutaceae	*Zanthoxylum naranjillo*	1	
Urticaceae	*Urera caracasana*	1	

Transect 7 - 130 x 10 m

27 May 1995. First ridge to the north of Río Santa Martha. 20°41'55"S, 64°18'43"W. 1300 m elevation. Tall (20-25 m), semi-deciduous cloudforest on ridgetop.

Family	Genus, species	Number of individuals >10 cm dbh in transect	Number of trees >30 cm dbh in transect (in parentheses)
Meliaceae	*Trichilia clausseni*	24	
Myrtaceae	*Siphoneugena occidentalis*	16	(5)
Rosaceae	*Prunus integrifolia*	7	(1)
Sapindaceae	*Diatenopterix sorbifolia*	7	
Bignoniaceae	*Tabebuia lapacho*	6	(2)
Lauraceae		5	
Olacaceae	*Ximenia americana*	5	
Proteaceae	*Roupala montana*	5	(2)
Sapindaceae	*Cupania vernalis*	4	(1)
Fabaceae	*Myroxylon peruiferum*	3	(3)
Euphorbiaceae	*Croton urucurana*	2	(2)
Melastomataceae	*Miconia calvescens,* probably	2	
Sapotaceae	*Chrysophyllum gonocarpum*	2	
Verbenaceae	*Aegiphila saltensis*	2	
Aquifoliaceae	*Ilex argentina*	1	(1)
Boraginaceae	*Cordia alliodora*	1	
Elaeocarpaceae	*Muntingia calabura* ?	1	
Fabaceae	*Machaerium* sp.	1	
Icacinaceae	*Citronella apogon*	1	
Lauraceae		1	(1)
Meliaceae	*Cedrela lilloi*	1	(1)
Rutaceae	*Citrus aurantium*	1	
Sapindaceae	*Cupania vernalis*	1	
Tiliaceae	*Luehea fiebrigii*	1	

Transect 8 - 65 x 10 m

29 May 1995. Cerro Los Tigrecillos, summit on western edge, north of Río Santa Martha. 20°39'21"S, 64°20'22"W. 2150 m elevation. Low (5-8 m) semi-deciduous cloudforest near edge of mesa.

Family	Genus, species	Number of individuals >10 cm dbh in transect	Number of trees >30 cm dbh in transect (in parentheses)
Aquifoliaceae	*Ilex argentina*	33	
Clethraceae	*Clethra* aff. *scabra*	29	
Symplocaceae	*Symplocos* aff. *subcuneata*	23	
Caprifoliaceae	*Viburnum seemenii*	15	

Transect 9 - 112 x 10 m

29 May 1995. Cerro Los Tigrecillos, summit on western edge, north of Río Santa Martha. 20°39'21"S, 64°20'22"W. 2150 m elevation. Medium (10-15 m) semi-deciduous cloudforest on gently undulating terrain.

Family	Genus, species	Number of individuals >10 cm dbh in transect	Number of trees >30 cm dbh in transect (in parentheses)
Clethraceae	*Clethra* aff. *scabra*	29	
Caprifoliaceae	*Viburnum seemenii*	21	
Aquifoliaceae	*Ilex argentina*	16	
Rosaceae	*Prunus tucumanensis*	12	(2)
Myrtaceae	*Myrcia* cf. *multiflora*	8	
Elaeocarpaceae	*Crinondendron tucumanum*	5	(2)
Lauraceae		5	(3)
Podocarpaceae	*Podocarpus parlatorei*	2	(2)
Rhamnaceae	*Rhamnus sphaerosperma*	2	

Transect 10 - 111 x 10 m

30 May 1995. First ridge to the north of Río Santa Martha. 20°40'55"S, 64°19'29"W. 1500 m elevation. Tall (20-25 m) semi-deciduous cloudforest on ridgetop.

Family	Genus, species	Number of individuals >10 cm dbh in transect	Number of trees >30 cm dbh in transect (in parentheses)
Rutaceae	*Citrus aurantium*	35	
Myrtaceae	*Siphoneugena occidentalis*	15	(2)
Bignoniaceae	*Tabebuia lapacho*	9	(3)
Aquifoliaceae	*Ilex argentina*	8	(8)
Rosaceae	*Prunus* sp.	5	(1)
Myrtaceae	*Myrcia* sp.	4	
Proteaceae	*Roupala meisneri*	4	
Verbenaceae	*Aegiphila saltensis*	4	
Lauraceae	*Phoebe porphyria*	3	(1)
Melliaceae	*Trichilia clausseni*	3	
Euphorbiaceae	*Croton urucurana*	2	(2)
Lauraceae	*Ocotea* sp. 3	1	(1)
Lauraceae	sp. 1	1	
Mimosaceae	*Inga* sp.	1	
Nyctaginaceae	*Pisonia ambigua*	1	
Sapindaceae	*Cupania vernalis*	1	
Sapotaceae	*Chrysophyllum gonocarpum*	1	
Solanaceae	*Solanum* sp. 1	1	

Transect 11 - 140 x 10 m

30 May 1995. First ridge to the north of Río Santa Martha. 20°40'55"S, 64°19'29"W. ca. 1500 m elevation. Tall (20-25 m) semi-deciduous cloudforest on steep slope below ridge.

Family	Genus, species	Number of individuals >10 cm dbh in transect	Number of trees >30 cm dbh in transect (in parentheses)
Myrtaceae	*Siphoneugena occidentalis*	29	(5)
Myrtaceae	*Myrcia* sp.	24	(3)
Sapindaceae	*Cupania vernalis*	8	(4)
Bignoniaceae	*Tabebuia lapacho*	7	(4)
Verbenaceae	*Aegiphila saltensis*	7	
Melastomataceae	*Miconia* sp.	5	
Proteaceae	*Roupala meisneri*	5	
Aquifoliaceae	*Ilex argentina*	3	(1)
Rosaceae	*Prunus integrifolia*	3	
Lauraceae	sp. 2	2	(1)
?		1	
Euphorbiaceae	*Croton urucurana*	1	
Lauraceae		1	(1)
Lauraceae	"green petioles"	1	
Myrtaceae	*Myrciaria* cf. *floribunda*	1	
Rutaceae	*Citrus aurantium*	1	
Rutaceae	*Zanthoxylum* sp.	1	

Birds of Cerro Bufete and the Río Santa Martha Basin, South Central Chuquisaca, Bolivia

Thomas S. Schulenberg, Carmen Quirroga O., and Lois Jammes

	Habitats	Cerro Bufete	Santa Martha	Evidence
TINAMIDAE (2)				
Rhynchotus maculicollis	H	R		si
Crypturellus tataupa	Fe		R	si
ARDEIDAE (1)				
Tigrisoma fasciatum	Rm		R	ph
ANATIDE (1)				
Merganetta armata	Rm		R	si
CATHARTIDAE (2)				
Cathartes aura	O	U	U	si
Vultur gryphus	O	R		si
ACCIPITRIDAE (2)				
Buteo polyosoma	O	R		si
Spizastur melanoleucus	Fm	R		si
FALCONIDAE (1)				
Micrastur ruficollis	Fsd		U	t
COLUMBIDAE (3)				
Columba fasciata	Fsf	U		si
Leptoptila megalura	Fm		U	t
Geotrygon frenata	Fm	U		si
PSITTACIDAE (5)				
Ara militaris	Fsd		R	t
Aratinga mitrata	Fm, Fsd	F	F	t
Pyrrhura molinae	Fm	F	F	t
Pionus maximiliani	Fsd		F	si
Amazona aestiva	Fsd		F	t
CUCULIDAE (1)				
Piaya cayana	Fm, Fsd	F	F	si
STRIGIDAE (4)				
Otus hoyi	Fm	F		t
Glaucidium jardinii	Fm	U		si
Glaucidium brasilianum	Fsd		U	si
Ciccaba (albitarsus)	Fm		U	t

	Habitats	Cerro Bufete	Santa Martha	Evidence
CAPRIMULGIDAE (1)				
Caprimulgus longirostris	Fe	U		si
APODIDAE (1)				
Aeronautes montivagus	O	U		si
TROCHILIDAE (7)				
Phaethornis pretrei	Fm, Fsd	F	F	t
Thalurania furcata	Fm	U		t
Amazilia chionogaster	Fe	R		si
Adelomyia melanogenys	Fm	F	F	t
Eriocnemis glaucopoides	Fm	F		t
Sappho sparganura	Fe, Sh	U		t
Microstilbon burmeisteri	Fe	R		si
TROGONIDAE (2)				
Trogon curucui	Fm	R		si
Trogon personatus	Fm		U	t
ALCEDINIDAE (1)				
Ceryle torquata	Rm		U	si
RAMPHASTIDAE (1)				
Ramphastos toco	Fsd	U	U	si
PICIDAE (5)				
Picumnus cirrhatus	Fm	U		t
Veniliornis frontalis	Fsd	U		si
Veniliornis fumigatus	Fm	F		si
Piculus rubiginosus	Fm, Fsd	U	U	t
Campephilus melanoleucos	Fm, Fsd		U	t
DENDROCOLAPTIDAE (1)				
Sittasomus griseicapillus	Fm	U	U	si
FURNARIIDAE (8)				
Cinclodes fuscus	Rm	U	U	si
Leptasthenura fuliginiceps	Fsf	R		si
Synallaxis azarae superciliosa	Fm	F	F	t
Poecilurus scutatus	Fsd		U	t
Asthenes heterura	Fsf, Fe	F		si
Asthenes punensis	Sh	R		si

Habitats

Fm	Montane semi-decidudous forest
Fsd	Semideciduous forest
Fsf	Evergreen shrub forest
Fo	Forest openings
Fe	Forest edge
Sh	Shrub / meadow mosaic
H	Herbaceous meadows
Rm	River margins
O	Overhead

Abundance

F	Fairly common
U	Uncommon
R	Rare

Evidence

t	Tape
si	Species ID by sight
ph	Photograph

	Habitats	Cerro Bufete	Santa Martha	Evidence
Syndactyla rufosuperciliata	Fm, Fsf	F	F	t
Xenops rutilans	Fsd		U	si
FORMICARIIDAE (5)				
Thamnophilus caerulescens	Fm	U	U	t
Thamnophilus ruficapillus	Fsf	R		t
Herpsilochmus atricapillus	Fsd		U	t
Grallaria albigula	Fm	U		t
Conopophaga ardesiaca	Fm	U	U	si
RHINOCRYPTIDAE (3)				
Melanopareia maximiliani	Sh	R		t
Scytalopus bolivianus	Fm	U	F	t
Scytalopus superciliaris zimmeri	Sh	R		t
PIPRIDAE (1)				
Chiroxiphia boliviana	Fm	R	U	t
TYRANNIDAE (15)				
Phyllomyias burmeisteri	Fm	R		si
Phyllomyias sclateri	Fsd	F		si
Elaenia (parvirostris)	Fsf	R		si
Mecocerculus leucophrys	Fm	F	F	t
Mionectes striaticollis	Fm	U		t
Leptopogon amaurocephalus	Fsd	U		si
Phylloscartes ventralis	Fm	F	F	t
Todirostrum plumbeiceps	Fm	U	U	t
Tolmomyias sulphurescens	Fm, Fsd	U	U	t
Contopus fumigatus	Fm		U	t
Sayornis nigricans	Rm		U	si
Myiarchus tyrannulus	Fsd	U		si
Myiotheretes striaticollis	Sh	U		t
Agriornis microptera	H	R		si
Hirundinea ferruginea	Fo	F		si
HIRUNDINIDAE (1)				
Notiochelidon cyanoleuca	O	F		si
MOTACILLIDAE (1)				
Anthus hellmayri	H	U		t

	Habitats	Cerro Bufete	Santa Martha	Evidence
CORVIDAE (2)				
Cyanocorax chrysops	Fsd		U	t
Cyanocorax cyanomelas	Fm, Fsd	U	U	t
CINCLIDAE (1)				
Cinclus schulzi	Rm	U	U	si
TROGLODYTIDAE (2)				
Troglodytes aedon	Fe	U	U	t
Troglodytes solstitialis	Fm	F	F	t
TURDIDAE (6)				
Catharus dryas	Fm	U	U	t
Turdus amaurochalinus	Fe	R		si
Turdus chiguanco	Fe, Fsf	F		t
Turdus nigriceps	Fm	R		si
Turdus rufiventris	Fsf	R		si
Turdus serranus	Fm	U	U	t
VIREONIDAE (1)				
Cyclarhis gujanensis	Fm, Fsd	U	F	t
EMBERIZINAE (7)				
Zonotrichia capensis	H, Fe	U		t
Poospiza erythrophrys	Fsf	F		t
Sicalis sp.	H	R		si
Sporophila sp.	Fe	R		si
Arremon flavirostris	Fsd	F		si
Atlaptetes fulviceps	Fsf	F		t
Atlapetes torquatus	Fm, Fsd	F	F	t
CARDINALINAE (2)				
Pheucticus aureoventris	Fsd	U		t
Cyanocompsa brissonii	Fsd	U	U	t
THRAUPINAE (7)				
Chlorospingus ophthalmicus	Fm	F	F	t
Piranga leucoptera	Fm	U	U	t
Thraupis sayaca	Fe	R		si
Anisognathus flavinucha	Fm	U		t
Pipraeidea melanonota	Fsd	U	F	t

Habitats

Fm	Montane semi-decidudous forest
Fsd	Semideciduous forest
Fsf	Evergreen shrub forest
Fo	Forest openings
Fe	Forest edge
Sh	Shrub / meadow mosaic
H	Herbaceous meadows
Rm	River margins
O	Overhead

Abundance

F	Fairly common
U	Uncommon
R	Rare

Evidence

t	Tape
si	Species ID by sight
ph	Photograph

	Habitats	Cerro Bufete	Santa Martha	Evidence
Chlorophonia cyanea	Fm	R		t
Diglossa baritula	Fe	U		si
PARULIDAE (4)				
Parula pitiayumi	Fsd	F	F	t
Myioborus brunneiceps	Fsd, Fm	F	F	t
Basileuterus bivittatus	Fsd, Fm	F	F	t
Basileuterus signatus	Fm	F	F	t
ICTERIDAE (2)				
Psarocolius decumanus	Fsd		U	t
Cacicus chrysopterus	Fm	F		t

Preliminary List of the Mammals of Bosque Tucumano-Boliviano

Louise H. Emmons

This list encompasses the mammalian species recorded from the moist forests between about 900 m and 3000 m on the eastern Andean slope, from about 18° S in southern Cochabamba, Bolivia, south to about 24° S in Jujuy, Argentina.

The list follows the taxonomy in Wilson and Reeder (1992), especially for rodents (Musser and Carleton 1992), with geographic range notes, and is derived from the following principal sources: Argentina: Olrog (1979; ref. 1), Ojeda and Mares (1989; ref. 2); Bolivia: Anderson (1993; ref. 3), specimens in USNM (ref. 4); Myers (1989; ref. 5); and this study (ref. 6). Some names have been changed to conform to recent usage. There are many unanswered taxonomic problems, and there is uncertainty about taxonomic classification due to recent taxonomic changes. Likewise, the region is poorly inventoried, and additional species can be expected. ( ) = lowland species probably marginal in the designated elevational range.

	Geographic Range[1]		Reference
MARSUPIALIA			
Didelphidae			
Didelphis albiventris	3		1, 2
Lutreolina crassicaudata	3 (1?)		1, 2, 6
Micoureus constantiae budini	1		1, 2, 3, 6
(Thylamys elegans)	3		2, 3
Thylamys pallidior	3		1, 3
CHIROPTERA			
Noctilionidae			
Noctilio leporinus	3		2
Phyllostomidae			
Chrotopterus auritus	3		1, 2
Glossophaga soricina	3		1, 2
Anoura caudifera	3		2, 6
Anoura geoffroyi	3		6
(Artibeus planirostris)	3		1, 2, 6
(Artibeus lituratus)	3		2
Pygoderma bilabiatum	3		2
Sturnira erythromos	3		3, 6
Sturnira lilium	3		1, 2
Desmodus rotundus	3		1, 2, 6
Diaemus youngi	3		2

	Geographic Range[1]		Reference
Vespertilionidae			
Eptesicus furinalis	3		2
Lasiurus blossvillei	3		1, 2, 6
Lasiurus cinereus	3		2
Molossidae			
Eumops perotis	3		2
Tadarida brasiliensis	3		2, 6
PRIMATES			
Cebidae			
Cebus apella	3		1, 2, 6
XENARTHRA			
Myrmecophagidae			
Tamandua tetradactyla	3		2
CARNIVORA			
Canidae			
Cerdocyon thous	3		1, 2
Lycalopex culpaeus	3		2
Ursidae			
Tremarctos ornatus	3		3, 6
Procyonidae			
Procyon cancrivorus	3		1, 2
Nasua nasua	3		1
Galictis cuja	3		1
Mustelidae			
Eira barbara	3		1, 2, 6
Lontra longicaudis	3		1, 2, 6
Conepatus chinga	3		1
Felidae			
Oncifelis colocolo	3		1
Herpailurus yaguarondi	3		1
Leopardus wiedii	3		1
Panthera onca	3		1, 2, 6
Puma concolor	3		1, 2, 6

	Geographic Range[1]		Reference
PERISSODACTYLA			
Tapiridae			
Tapirus terrestris	3		1, 2, 6
ARTIODACTYLA			
Tayassuidae			
(Tayassu tajacu)	3		1
Cervidae			
Mazama americana	3		1, 2, 6?
RODENTIA			
Sciuridae			
Sciurus argentineus	1		1, 2, 6
Muridae			
Akodon albiventer	2		1, 2, 3
Akodon (Hypsimys) budini	1		1, 4, 6
Akodon fumeus	2		3, 6
Akodon siberiae	1		3
Akodon sylvanus	1		3
Akodon simulator	1		3
Akodon varius	1		2
(Calomys callosus)	3		1
Graomys domorum	1		2
Holochilus brasiliensis	3		2
Oecomys mamorae	3		4
Oligoryzomys cf. *destructor*	3		4?, 6
Oligoryzomys longicaudatus	3		2, 3
Oligoryzomys nigripes	3		6
Oryzomys legatus	1		2, 3, 4
(Oryzomys nitidus)	3		6
Oxymycterus inca	2		4, 6
Oxymycterus paramensis	2		1, 2, 4
Phyllotis wolffsohni	1		4
Rhipidomys austrinus	1		1, 4
Rhipidomys leucodactylus	3		2, 6

	Geographic Range[1]		Reference
Dasyproctidae			
Dasyprocta cf. *variegata*	3		1, 2, 6
Ctenomyidae			
Ctenomys frater ssp.	1		1, 2
LAGOMORPHA			
Leporidae			
Silvilagus brasiliensis	3		1, 2

[1] Geographic range loosely divided into three categories: 1 = confined to Andean slopes between southern Cochabamba, Bolivia and Jujuy, Argentina; 2 = confined to Andean slopes from southeastern Peru to southern Bolivia or northern Argentina; 3 = wider ranging.

TAXONOMIC NOTES

Lutreolina crassicaudata: Olrog (1979) commented that specimens collected in Andean forests in Jujuy were of small body size and probably represented an unnamed subspecies. As far as we know, this idea has not been studied further. Specimens from the Andes also seem to have a different color than do lowland forms. The Andean populations certainly deserve a critical evaluation, especially since the habitat they occupy, of rushing mountain streams in forest above 1000 m, is quite different from the typical habitat of lowland flooded grasslands outside of forests. The two specimens we collected are juveniles, and thus do not shed light on this question.

Micoureus constantiae budini: The specimens we collected seem distinct in pelage characters from the lowland forms of the genus (*Micoureus constantiae constantiae*). The genus needs taxonomic revision.

Sciurus argentineus (Thomas 1921): We assign our specimens from Chuquisaca to this species, which has Jujuy as the type locality and is the only species in that region of Argentina. In Argentine publications it is listed as *S. ignitus*. *Sciurus argentineus* is unlike, both externally and cranially, any of the geographically closest squirrels (*S. spadiceus, S. ignitus, S. aestuans*). It is almost impossible to understand why it was considered a synonym of *S. ignitus*, as it shares no distinguishing characters with specimens of that species group. Our specimens differ in color from the description of the type of *S. argentinius*, but skull measurements are very close (and unlike those of any other species in South America). When he described it, Thomas (1921) noted that it was most similar to *Sciurus granatensis hoffmanni* (from Costa Rica and Andean Colombia), a taxon notorious for dramatic geographic differences in color. The Andean endemic squirrel *S. pyrrhinus*, from central Peru, also has been considered part of the same genus/subgenus as *S. granatensis* ssp. The skulls of both of these species, as represented in the collections of the USNM, are much larger than, although of similar shape to, the *S. argentineus* specimens from near El Palmar, and the three may constitute a clade. Molecular comparisons from tissues of our specimens are underway (by V. L. Roth and J. Mercer), which may help to resolve this question.

Mammals of the Río Urucuti Basin, South Central Chuquisaca, Bolivia

Louise H. Emmons

Species that were collected are indicated with an asterisk (*). 'T' denotes species that were detected only by their tracks.

	BUFETE 2050 m	LIMÓN 900 m	TIGRECILLO 2150 m
OPOSSUMS			
Lutreolina cf. crassicaudata	X*		
Micoureus constantiae budini	X*	X*	
ARMADILLOS			
Dasypus novemcinctus	(in valley of El Palmar)		
BATS			
Anoura caudifera		X*	
Anoura geoffroyi	X*		
Artibeus planirostris		X*	
Sturnira erythromos			X*
Desmodus rotundus		X*	
Lasiurus blossvillei			X*
Tadarida brasiliensis	X*		
PRIMATES			
Cebus apella		X	
CARNIVORES			
Eira barbara		X	
Felis sp.		T	
Lycalopex sp.		T	
Lontra longicaudis		T	
Panthera onca		T	
Puma concolor		T	
Tremarctos ornatus		T	T
TAPIR			
Tapirus terrestris		T	T

MAMMALS OF THE RÍO URUCUTI BASIN, SOUTH CENTRAL CHUQUISACA, BOLIVIA

	BUFETE 2050 m	LIMÓN 900 m	TIGRECILLO 2150 m
DEER			
Mazama sp.	(in valley of El Palmar)		
RODENTS			
Sciurus argentineus	X	X*	
Akodon (Hypsimys) sp.	X*		
Akodon fumeus	X*		
Akodon cf. *siberiae*	X*		
Akodon sp.	X*		
Ctenomys (burrows)	X		
Oligoryzomys nigripes	X*		
Oligoryzomys destructor		X*	
Oryzomys nitidus		X*	
Oxymycteris inca	X*		
Rhipidomys cf. *leucodactylus*	X*	X*	
Dasyprocta cf. *variegata*		X	

Reptiles and Amphibians of the Bosque Tucumano-Boliviano and adjacent deforested areas of Chuquisaca

Michael B. Harvey

Species not previously reported from Bolivia are indicated by an asterisk.

Species	Habitat
ANURA	
Bufonidae	
Bufo veraguensis	Mountain stream
Bufo sp. 1 * (*B. marinus* group *sensu* Duellman and Schulte 1992; possibly *B. gallardoi*)	Wet forest
Bufo sp. 2 (*B. typhonius* group *sensu* Duellman and Schulte 1992)	Wet forest
Centrolenidae	
Cochranella bejaranoi	Mountain stream
Hylidae	
Gastrotheca marsupiata	Wet forest
Hyla armata	Mountain stream
Hyla callipleura/Hyla marianitae [1]	Mountain stream
Hyla minuta	El Palmar valley
Hyla pulchella/Hyla varelae [2]	El Palmar valley
Scinax castroviejoi	El Palmar valley
Leptodactylidae	
Eleutherodactylus discoidalis	Wet forest
Leptodactylus chaquensis	El Palmar valley
Leptodactylus gracilis *	El Palmar valley
Odontophrynus americanus	Forest edge
Telmatobius simonsi	El Palmar valley, Montane meadows, Mountain stream
Microhylidae	
Elachistocleis ovalis	El Palmar valley
SQUAMATA	
Colubridae	
(new species) * [3]	Montane meadows
Chironius exoletus	Forest edge

REPTILES AND AMPHIBIANS OF THE BOSQUE TUCUMANO-BOLIVIANO AND ADJACENT DEFORESTED AREAS OF CHUQUISACA

Species	Habitat
Liophis ceii	El Palmar valley
Liophis sagittifer	El Palmar valley
Liophis typhlus	El Palmar valley
Oxyrhopus rhombifer	Forest edge
Philodryas psammophideus	El Palmar valley
Philodryas varius	Montane meadows
Waglerophis merremii	Forest edge
Gymnophthalmidae	
Opipeuter xestus	Wet forest, Montane meadows
Pantodactylus schreibersi parkeri	El Palmar valley
Tropiduridae	
Liolaemus sp.* [3]	El Palmar valley
Stenocercus marmoratus	Montane meadows
Stenocercus caducus	Wet forest
Tropidurus melanopleurus	Rock outcrops along Río Santa Martha
Viperidae	
Bothrops neuwiedi	El Palmar valley

[1] In its original description (Carrizo 1992), *Hyla marianitae* was not compared to its very similar congener *Hyla callipleura* or to any other species of *Hyla*. Because of its inadequate description, *Hyla marianitae* can not be distinguished from *Hyla callipleura* without the examination of comparative material. Further study is required to determine whether these specimens from Chuquisaca represent an undescribed species, *Hyla callipleura*, or *Hyla marianitae*. The last species has not been reported previously from Bolivia.

[2] *Hyla varelae* was not compared to its very similar congener *Hyla pulchella* in its original description (Carrizo 1992). I tentatively assign these specimens from Chuquisaca to the latter species.

[3] New species. An apparently undescribed species of *Liolaemus* and an obviously new species of colubrid snake are each known only from two specimens and represent new records for the country.